IN LOVING MEMORY

LINDA SUE ORLANDO

Galactic Herstory

Vol. I

Tales of a Warrior Born by the Light

Gina Orlando

ISBN: 978-1-7369838-0-5 (paperback)

Cover and Interior Design: Mark Moshier and Gina Orlando

Formatting and Editing: Aaron Rose, Mount Shasta, California

Artwork by Gina Orlando

For more information, please visit www.sacredemergence.com.

Mythic Art, Poetry, Dreams, Vision

a love story of creation
dedicated to the Great Mother
and the children of humanity

Contents

PART I: THE FALL...

PART 2: THE RISE...

PART 3: THE BECOMING...

Acknowledgements

To my Mother: What can I say…you always were the catalyst
to my ultimate becoming. May you rest in eternal peace. 241.

To my Father: Thank you for encouraging my uniqueness
and supporting me to realize my dream. So much love and gratitude.

To my precious Body: Thank you, dear beloved, for carrying me
on this Earth walk. I am so very grateful to you
for your unconditional love, support, wisdom, and healing teachings.

To the Spirits of the Stars and these Lands: I am truly humbled
by the grace of your presence. Thank you for sharing your noble truths,
trusting me with your voice, and guiding me home to where I belong.

To all my fellow Travelers who have challenged and inspired me along the way:
I thank you from the bottom of my heart.
I have learned so very much from each and every one of you.

A special thanks to Aaron and Violet for midwifing this book to life.
Thank you for believing in the possibility and having the vision to see.
So much love and gratitude.

To all the Travelers, Dreamers, Healers, Artists, Visionaries:
Keep on believing, because dreams really do come true.

To my Knight in shining armor and our beautiful feline Goddess Queen:
Thank you. I love you.
This could not have been possible without the two of you.

To the Great Spirit, the One Infinite Creator:
Words can not express my emotion…
Thank you for birthing this beautiful world into being,
for giving us the opportunity to learn, heal, and grow,
to love, laugh…to create beauty in the world,
to live our dream,
and to remember ourselves
home to you…

How to Use This Book

Dear Beloved One,

This is an invitation to travel deep within…this is a book of poetry
that reads like a narrative. It is timelessness in nature.
It is separated into three sections: *The Fall, The Rise,* and *The Becoming.*
The Fall is about surrender, initiation, awakening to life,
confrontation of the shadow, and forgiveness.
The Rise is about choices, initiating change, developing courage,
and finding the will power to step forward.
The Becoming is about the return home, alchemical marriage, embodiment,
acceptance, and completion.

This book can be used as an oracle by asking a question and then flipping
randomly to a page for guidance, or you can simply read it cover to cover.
You may choose to read certain poems out loud to feel the energy in motion
moving through your body, or you may choose to pause for deep thought
and reflection after each writing or section.
You may decide to keep a journal nearby in case something stirs in you
that needs to be witnessed or clarified, or maybe even elaborated upon.

I invite you to drop into your heart…brew a hot cup of tea such as blue lotus,
rose, or damiana, and if you really want to get crazy you can blend your
brewed tea with some cacao and top with honey for a yummy cacao elixir.
Find a cozy spot in Nature, maybe outside in your garden, at your favorite
park under a tree, by a river stream, or deep in the woods.
Listen to the spirits of the stars and the land all around you.
You may notice signs or synchronicities;
plant or animal spirits may randomly appear as you read along.
Or you may choose to build a nest, a sacred quiet space inside your home,
with some warm blankets and pillows, to go deep within.
You may light a fire or a beeswax candle, light some incense,
or diffuse an essential oil such as rose, jasmine, or nutmeg.
Sip slowly, breathe deeply…drop in, tune in, hum a melody…
The Love Story of Creation.

May this book enchant your life as it has done mine
and inspire you to create a vision of your wildest dreams.
Blessed be you, dear Star Traveler. Aho!

Introduction

I came into this world with a keen sense of awareness.
I remembered I was a Star Traveler from another Universe
and that I was not the only one.
We were each called forth for our unique talents and abilities
for a very important mission:
to help heal our beloved Mother Earth.
I remembered I was an Elder Spirit of the Ancient One,
an artist, storyteller, dreamweaver,
a Shaman of Creation.
But then something happened…

I lost my balance and fell,
and when I fell, my soul shattered into a billion pieces;
only shards of glass remained.
I wish I could say that was my only fall, but the truth is,
once I fell, I kept on falling until I could no longer fall.
I sank down into a bottomless pit of nothingness
until I arrived at what I came to understand as the Void of Creation.
I heard Her call to me from the ashes…our Mother of Holy Grace.

She spoke to me in an ancient tongue, a dialect I remembered from eons past.
I cried out to her, "Mother: please, this is too much to bear."
She told me I would need to learn to be a part of this world
or to forever be consumed by its wrath.

She reminded me that I was here to help humanity evolve in consciousness
without losing its emotion.
She shared with me about our galactic roots,
our ancient past and promised future.
She reminded me that I was a Warrior Spirit of the Blue Dragon Tribe
and that I came in loving service to heal a very ancient bloodline.

She told me that the only way to heal
was to feel all the pain and suffering from eons past
and to learn how to transform that energy
into love and beauty.

She went on to say that this was not personal but universal
and that this experience was not meant to punish
but to liberate humanity from its karmic past.
She reminded me of how she gifted each of us with a unique song
and that it was up to us to discover the tune.
It took me many years of deep listening and silence to discover this tune,
to re-member who I was and what I was made of.

I began to speak in this Mother tongue, dance and sing the ancestor song,
and drum the Heartbeat of the Universe.
I never planned on writing a book,
but I soon discovered that a cosmic story was being birthed through me.
It was a living story that wanted to be seen, heard, felt,
remembered by one and all.
I began to translate this language of light
into art, music, poetry, dance, dreams, vision.
It began to heal my wounds
and integrate my knowing and wisdom from eons past.

I received my gift...I became a temple of living light,
the embodiment of the flame and the creation song.
And now this gift I give to you, dear reader,
to share with you what I have learned from my travels and woes.
To share with you a story of enchantment
and deep remembrance of who we are and what we are made of.

If you are reading this, then you too are an Elder Spirit of the Ancient One,
a Shaman of Creation.
I honor you, my dear beloved, oh radiant one!
May this book be a beacon of light and sound,
to activate your ancient memories
and inspire you to step forward in divine grace,
to share your voice and your unique song.

Prologue

It is said that in every age since the Dawn of Creation
there have been angels and demons that have helped guide humanity
to its doom or bloom.
Our present age happens to be a time of reconciliation,
a time when we would finally face our fears, settle our differences,
and integrate our knowledge and wisdom from eons past.
Human vessels are the transformers of these sacred teachings,
alchemizing lead into gold, pure crystalline light.

You see, we are an ancient family, birthed from the Divine Sun and Moon.
We are each a son and daughter of this sacred flame…
parents and guardians of creation.
This story is a fierce tale of the collision of these two forces
and the birth of something new, completely unimaginable…Freedom.
We transcend fear and liberate the mind.
You see, we are each born out of love,
and then we return to love in our own way and time,
but some of us forget, we lose hope along the way,
so we need reminders from those that still remember the way forward.

This tale is about re-membering who we are and what we are made of.
It's not easy, and it's not always pretty, but we persevere…
Heroes of Night, Warriors of Light, we sound the way forward.
We return one by one into the Collective Force of Source,
sharing tales of our travels and woes,
healing through the ripples of time,
becoming truly human, divinely crafted by the sign of faith.
These writings are messages from the Divine,
transcribed through the unique lens of my human experience.
I believe this is a gift that we all share…the art of storytelling,
making sense of the senseless through our art, music, dance, dreams…vision.
And so, this is a living story…it is our story.
The Love Story of Creation…we sing it, dream it, feel it together.

Dear Starseed

I am humbled by the grace of your presence…
your love, song, beauty.
How do we keep the essence alive?
We weave it into the tapestry, one of many…
it becomes…it blooms into greatness.
We are all the magicians of our kingdom.

Some are dreamers…we are the engineers, architects,
interior designers of the internal structure.
One can not exist without the other.
We need a foundation if the world is to grow.

If we can bring order to our internal chaos,
we can exhibit balance in the external infrastructure as well.
Ignore the lie, feed the truth.
Please feed your soul!

The Summons

It is time to kneel and pray,
to sit with the Earth, to acknowledge her call.
We are all being called, gathered, initiated.
It is time…time to rise.
We can do this for our Mother Earth.
Sisters and Brothers, I call on you.
Mother needs us. It's time to kneel and pray.
Lift our hearts and rise to the beat of our own drum.
Music to my ears. Please sing your song!

The Beginning

Since history seems to always be rewritten by the victors,
I decided to seize an opportunity.
This story is not about who I am, but rather a story of who I became…
I had a dream that became a vision that spun into a reality.
In the beginning there was love,
and in the ending we found our way back home…to love.
And so, we begin again as the starring roles in Her story.

Mythic Journey

It all began with a dream, a vision for humanity.
We are the realization of that dream.
We are many authors and one book, many voices and one song.
We are all here to save the world.
We each have our own mythic journey which together unite as one epic.
We are heroes on a quest for truth.
We slay the dragon, gather our lost parts, and find the elixir to nourish our soul.
We become the dragon…we re-member ourselves home.

We are each the sacred medicine-holder of the wisdom of our temple body.
We hold the key to re-discovering that which has been hidden from us long ago.
Through soulful inquiry and embodied practice,
we can begin to heal core wounds and ancestral trauma that has kept us small
and from embracing the truth of who we are.
As we begin to recover these lost lands, we reclaim our roots
and our sense of belonging in the world.
With a strong sense of self and embodied presence, we then have the power
to seed our dream into the collective dream of humanity
and heal our beloved Mother Earth.

This is one soul's mythic journey of becoming…truly human.
It is a journey through the sacred portal of the otherworld.
This is a magical kingdom where all life is animated.
It is a place in between the mundane physical world
and the Great Mystery beyond…

I believe this is the realm of soul and dreams.
It is timeless and spacious.
Patterns of energy, color, shape, sound, music to my ears.
This is where dreams are made, songs are sung, and creations are landed
into the hearts and souls of those who dare to dream
and manifest the imaginal into the mundane.

Could this be Sophia, our Root Mother, calling us home to our ancestors,
the natural world before it became the aftermath of a tall world order?
Just one day missed in Nature and consumed by this virtual reality
can be enough to drive anyone mad.

Are we merely patients locked in a mental institution, an insane asylum,
patiently awaiting our great escape?
Who are "they" to have power over us?

Contain the authorities, so we can set our souls free! Sing your song!
When we make the return back to Nature, back to our roots,
we remember who we are and why we are here:
Love.

There's no need to push...just Be centered and Free!

The time has come...hum hum hum woo...
the dragon meets the fly and births a Violet Flame,
a whimsical iridescence of Golden Light.
The Night descends...beauty ascends.
The Makers of an era, we rise to our call...

She felt him inside her...
wet dreams, deep longings, an explosion into their wildest dream.
He enters her...She receives him...
they then perceive reality through the lens of the One Eye.

And now, we enter here...

Initiation

It was a long, dark, cold night as I began my descent into the underworld.
A path few choose to travel, a path I must take
if I wish to retrieve a part of my soul that has been lost.
As I canoe down the murky river, I encounter some fellow travelers
who are overcome by fear and start to desperately paddle back upstream.

I take a deep breath and manage to navigate around them.
I muster up enough strength to get to dry land
where I encounter a huge black snake.
She raises her face to meet mine and hisses,
"Conquer the suffering so you can heal.
You are a Guardian of the Earth, and your healing accounts for billions."

"So how do I heal?" I ask.

"Well, my child, through patience, love, and kindness,
just like you would give to any other being.
Find your voice, and you will find your grace."

As I glance back at the snake, I see her begin spiraling into a double helix.
Then with a burst of light she is transformed into the sacred bird
the Ancient Phoenix.
This majestic bird appears to be holding a gift of some sort,
a small tightly wrapped package nestled inside a large gold ribbon.
As she extends her claw for me to receive this gift,
I feel my stomach begin to rumble and an intense purge coming on.

I kneel down to the ground and begin to cough up a thick slime
which seems to taste like tomato and basil.
Immediately, my mind is flooded with memories from childhood.
In sheer amazement I shout, "There, there it is,
my voice hidden deep within my gut in the root of my origin."
I let out a whistle to Firefly, my special winged friend, an all-white beauty,
strong as a horse and light as a feather.
She arrives just in time to whisk me away on a magical adventure…

I realize now this journey was an initiation into taking responsibility
for myself and not falling victim to the shadows of death.
In the shadows, in the darkness, is where we find our gift, the key to healing
the true part of Self we keep hidden away for fear of losing ourself.

3

Only when we risk the loss of ourself can we actually find ourself
and create wholeness.

To be whole is to be holy.
We are souls learning how to develop a relationship with our bodies,
aspiring to be human.
We have to learn how to be nothing before we can be something…
We are the medicine; life is the ritual.
It is in our absence that something is born…
We are the creators of our dream.

How can we be here when we are there?
Listen. Feel. Be. Presence…Light.
There is light in the darkness.
Re-member truth.

Mending the Sacred Hoop

Over the bridge and through the woods, off to Grandmother's house we go.
Down the rabbit hole and off to wonderland, off to lose our minds
and find our soul…

When we allow ourselves to be truly vulnerable with another human being,
we are able to bond.
That is where the healing happens and where the medicine is.
The medicine is called love. Freedom from mind control.
We find love through our process of healing and that of another.
Since we are all interconnected,
our healing journeys are intimately connected as well.
The illusion of fear has a strong hold on the mind
and triggers a trauma response when we least expect it.
When we respond with loving kindness, we "crack the code,"
break the pattern of this time loop.
We then move into a vibration of love.

Our wills are free, and we have the power to choose when we are ready
to move beyond, beyond the pain and suffering of this vicious cycle.
To bear witness to another's pain and suffering is just as challenging,
but we must honor their path with strength and compassion.
Through our presence they receive.
We can't give any more and nothing less.

We all have our unique role to play.
When we honor the gift of another, we self-accept, honoring our own divinity.
This allows freedom of creative expression to flow in the ocean of our hearts.
The power to create beauty in the world is a gift that we all share.
This is the ripple effect of our heart's song.

We can hear the melody through the voice of Nature.
Even in the silence it's always there.
The gentle hum of creation, a mere projection of our song.
To feel is love and to love is to be in harmony with our unique song.
We honor Self and accept what truly is…Love.

The Ritual

I dream I am taking a shower, preparing for ritual in a temple.
I am with other women. Not everyone is ready.
I have already felt the longing…the calling for this.
The Divine Mother is here. She is holding a child…a baby girl.
We all meet in a congregation room.

I am the first to hold the child.
She comes to me with open arms…we remember each other.
She is me and I am her.
There is a chair placed at the center of the circle
where each woman has an opportunity to hold and bond with this child.

Some say they are not ready or that they are already with child.
They miss an opportunity to experience this divine gift, this bond…
new life for the community.

Longing and Belonging

Our longing is to belong…we've been cast out of the circle and as a result
exiled ourselves from our sacred mandala temple-body and this land.
As if it's not punishment enough that we've been stripped of our ability
to bond with our own vessel, we've also been banished from the dream…

Our job is not to try to make everything better…
it is simply to witness, to experience, to be with, to hold…Presence.
Suffering is painful, grief is heavy, anger is throbbing, fear is paralyzing…
Feel it? Choices remind us we are free.

How do we know we are fully alive? We feel fully alive.
We create, we experience, we live, we learn, we laugh, we love, we dream,
we heal.

When we create, we seed life.
Our breath gives shape to form. It is expansive.
Other people try to change what they don't understand.
They think that control keeps them safe but it only keeps them small.
They try to hold us back by projecting their fears onto us,
acting like something is wrong with us. They can fix us, make us better.
Who are they?

In what world do we need someone to change us
so they can feel better about themselves?
Our pain and suffering give us depth of character.
It is a gift to truly know the depth of the human experience.
This is how we connect, bond.
The gift, the medicine, is we also get to experience love, joy, beauty,
pleasure, ecstasy.

Please don't take my pain away.
It is the only thing that keeps me sane in this insane asylum.
Ask for permission. Do not invade my space. Give me space to heal.
Hold your own so we can feel each other's company and enter in kinship
together as One.

The Starving Artist

We are part spirit and part matter. So we must attend to both needs.
Just as the physical body needs to drink water and eat food,
the soul also needs nourishment in order to survive and thrive.
Imagination, inspiration, and creativity feed the soul.
We are creative beings, each a unique expression of the One creative source.
We are each here to create life, to create beauty in the world.
It is our natural desire and our birthright.

What happens when our creative genius, life force, is blocked or misdirected?
It turns on us…we turn on each other like hungry ghosts feeding the lie,
the parasite infestation in our paradise.
Unexpressed creativity turns to destruction…dis-ease, addiction, greed,
manipulation, power, control…madness.

It is projected outward onto the masses, our relations, and humanity.
It is a lie that spreads like a virus infecting the meek.
This is not the truth we seek.

These are fragmented times we are living in,
and the paradox is that there is so much beauty and yet so much pain.
How do we hold both? I'm learning this through the art of comedy.
Transforming the larger picture into something people can relate to.
If they can relate, they can feel it.
We need people to feel so they can help carry some of the weight…heal.

Voice matters, speaking the word so people can hear, take notice, feel into it.
They are attracted to magnetism.
Give them what they want to feel, whole, and in return we feel a sense of unity,
even if it's only for a moment.
Moments matter. They add up, building a foundation,
a collection of new memories to override the trauma response.
We have to start somewhere.

It all begins here…
we are feeling into a New World with new hopes and dreams.
This is not easy, with no one to blame, no one holding us back.
Now, to face the awkward self and deal with the ego chanting,
"What if you fail? Who are you to achieve greatness?"
But we persevere…we can no longer deny the calling.
It is too strong, too loud. It awakens our sleep.
If we choose not to create art, beauty,
we are dead inside and dead outside as well.
"Oh my dear, but what if you fly?"
Do you believe?

The Rescue

I dream I am at the beach, swimming in the ocean…the waves are choppy.
I hear a baby crying. Nobody is around, and the baby is drowning.
I rescue the baby…we make it to shore and I give CPR.
Everyone is unaware of what just happened.
I am fearful of what may have happened to him.
I want to protect him.

I go to a circle of family who are unsupportive.
A shaman then appears, to take the baby back to the tribe.
The shaman looks me in the eyes and thanks me for saving the baby.
There is an understanding of mutual respect and power between us.

Returning to the Forest

Our evolution as a human species is dependent upon a revolution into love.
This is the solution to a convoluted system. Love is the solvent…

It is a miracle to be seeded into this creation.
Our will is strong if we made it through the birth canal,
but to continue to co-exist we must be in symbiotic relationship.
Even in the cosmos, in order to continue to create life
there is an order of giving and receiving energy, a sacred dance…
relationship.

The dream is still alive, but how can we thrive when our roots are perishing?
The council has spoken. Pretty soon we will cease to exist.
We need to open our eyes.
When will we see the damage we've done to our beloved Earth planet?
There is no room for blame…the shame game is over.
We've all played our part, and now, we need to own our part
by taking responsibility.

The only way to heal is to hurt…to feel the pain.
We must be willing to burn at the cross, stand our truth and ground,
rise to the beat of our own drum.
This is the revolution of our time. No more hiding…it is time.
Hearts blazing, fire in our eyes. See the light, see the smoke in the shadows.
Dust to dust, ashes to ashes. This is how we live our dream.

Keep creating, keep seeding love. Don't let them tear you down.
They can no longer defeat that which has already been defeated.
Remember this.
We hold the golden ticket and the key to our own destiny
they are just too blind to see.
We are the creators of our own reality. We must rise. We can do this!

Dear Mother

I feel your pain.
I know you feel the weight of the world,
and you want to make it better.
We are your children, and it's hard to watch us suffer.

I promise we are strong and will do our best to right a wrong.
We are in this together; please don't take all the blame.
We love you no matter what
and will be together someday soon,
near and far, far away...

The Calling

I felt myself being called out to the sea.
It was an intense calling that I could not deny.
I felt a deep longing...a yearning.
Suddenly, I realized I was naked and felt some fear wash over me
of feeling exposed...vulnerable.

I got in my car and drove to the end of the world.
I tried to find a parking space but couldn't find a spot anywhere.
It was as if I were in a maze...
every time I arrived I was led out deeper and deeper by the sea.

Bordering the sea were thick spiral vines resembling snakes.
There were signs that read "sacred waters" and "these vines are sacred."
I tried to turn around again to find a parking space...
my car got stuck in the vines,
and water swelled up into the vines.

I heard the waves thundering and roaring...my heart was pounding.
As I looked out to the sea, I saw waves crashing and surfers getting thrown
onto the rocky shores...slapped against the surface.
I wanted to help, but at the same time I was stuck...

Honoring the Call

Please sit down and shut the fudge up,
and please stand up and speak the fudge up!

Yes, you all know who you are. Thank you for understanding.
When we deny our gift, we deny our very spark for life itself.
Can you hear the gentle whisper calling you from deep within?
Shhh…Listen…Hear your call. Respond with loving kindness.
Embody the knowing you are.

You are the light, the understanding we need to cultivate, to grow, to heal.
Tend your inner garden. Mend your sacred hoop. Fend your power.
Shine brightly, love deeply, live wholeheartedly.
Be the gift and the medicine that you already are.
We all need you.

Becoming the Crone

I am not sick, I am sensitive.
I am fully alive…feeling the weight and intensity of it all,
so be patient with me.
Excuse you for feeling uncomfortable with me.
It's ok, I feel your pain. It will pass if you let it.
If you hold on, it will eat you alive!

We can be heroes together. We are the same.
How we share our medicine makes us unique.
We all have much to learn from each other.
The world can be chaotic, but we can be safe by holding our center.
So, we don't live in fear and miss our experience…miss connection.
Connection keeps us safe.
Why do we fear what we need to keep us safe, to feel fully alive to thrive?

Because of the parasite infestation into our paradise.
A twisted way of being has us brainwashed.
If we learn to connect, we will be free.
Our greatest allies are our bodies.
We must develop a relationship with our bodies to share in this experience.

Our bodies are our greatest teachers.
They hold our secrets and our wisdom.
When we feel safe in our bodies, we don't feel the weight of the world.
It is still there, but we are not consumed by it.
We can bear witness and have compassion…

She broke me down and tore me apart piece by piece until I was nothing...
Slowly, piece by piece, She began to weave me back together again
into the woman I was always meant to become...
a woman who has the love to heal,
a woman who has the power to stand in truth,
and a woman who has the wisdom to make a difference in the world.
Suddenly, I was pregnant with possibility...

Two-Spirited

From stardust to Earth we begin our descent into matter.
Twirling in a symbiotic pool of fluid,
we engage in a sacred dance in the womb of our Mother,
where the elements Earth, Water, Fire, Air
are birthed into the alchemical being we call Self.

We are small, yet infinite beyond space and time.
We are spirit, we are matter. We are wisdom, we are will.
We are all, and yet, we are nothing. We are love, pure innocent love.
From Earth to stardust, we begin again...

We all have two spirits that exist inside of us
that are struggling to develop a relationship with each other.
The longer and harder we try to keep them apart
the more intense the struggle becomes,
hence our suffering.
These spirits are innocent like children,
and when we suffer it is their way of sending us a message.
They cry out for our attention,
for us to hear their pain and attend to their needs, our needs.

We can not begin to feel at peace with ourselves
until we acknowledge their presence.
When we hear their voices, we allow ourselves to find our own voice,
and when we hear their pain, we can then acknowledge our feelings
and remember that it is okay to feel.
When we find our voice, we find our grace;
and when we acknowledge our feelings, we can then begin to heal our pain.

When we heal ourselves, we heal the ancestral codes imprinted in our DNA.

When we heal the ancestral codes, we heal our children,
and when we heal our children, we heal the Earth.
This is how we create an involution of our soul, a revolution of our mind,
and ultimately an evolution as a human species.
This is how we can transcend suffering and heal the world!

Return with the Elixir

I dream a circle of travelers have gathered at the beach to do a healing.
They set up a crystal grid near the ocean.
Waves start rolling in. Someone shouts,
"Look at the chem trails. They're coming! We have to go."

I take two crystals from the grid, a clear quartz and an amethyst,
and throw them in the water. Then I run for the hills.
When we get to the mountain, we hold our ground, protecting our land.
Some of us die. I am not afraid. I choose to live. To fight.
If I am to die, I will die with a purpose.

I then encounter a medicine woman who gives me an amulet
to wear around my neck.
It is a glass bottle with a ruby-red potion in it
with a multi-colored string wrapped around it.
She says, "Here, this will help you." I'm not sure if I can trust her.
She goes on to say, "You may be caught in a dream within a dream.
This will help to seem less chaotic so you can balance between both worlds."
I understand now and graciously accept her offer.

There is a war, a revolution happening…
There is a secret society of rebels that have taken up camp in deserted cities.
They are waiting undercover…
at times they will stage their own deaths just to keep the dream alive.
The Mystery School is in their mind's eye
and within their secret society of common fellowship.

The more layers of skin they shed, the more of a threat, a target, they become
in this covert operation.
We know who they are, but they don't know who we are.
We are just a number to them and can be discarded at any moment
in the blink of an eye.
So mind yourself gracefully, and we will see the dawn of a new day.

Reclaiming our Roots

Set fire to fire. Let it be done. It is what it is.
We are all here because we are part of the solution.
It's only when we think we are part of the problem
that we become the problem.
I remember, I am not afraid. I know who you are. You are me and I am you.
We are the same, we were both wounded.
It's what we choose to do with our hurt that separates us.

We all have the power to transform our hurt into love, not war.
We must give our power back to the Earth if we are to co-exist.
If you choose not, we will banish you to where you came from.
It is done. The tribe has spoken. Hail Kali Ma, Great Mother Goddess!
The power of love will always defeat the love of power.

They are trying to seed their parasite into the dream.
They can not. This paradise is ours…we dreamed it and we will sustain it.
From Earth to Water, Water to Fire, Fire to Air.
The Wind, the Fire, the Ocean, the Earth, the Cosmos…these are all our allies.
Yes, we are that powerful. We have joined forces. Ha Ha. Try again, parasite.
See you later, alligator. Nice try, trickster. Ha Ha.
Got your number and your game code. Delete!

I know I hold the key. You can not enter here. I am one of many.
A Flame Keeper, a protector of sacred knowledge…wisdom.
You may ask, how does one come to such high regard?
It is that we are willing to sacrifice ourselves for this sacred wisdom.
I will not set fire to another, just so I will not burn…I choose to burn.
This passion is what separates us, but yet allows us to hold this sacred gift…
to heal.
We must heal if we are to have compassion for another human being.

It is our birthright. We must go on.
You can not destroy us.
You will try to divide us, separate us, with the very things we hold sacred.
Well, I say to thee, you have a choice…to stand with us or to die amongst us.
It can not be both. There is no middle way here. Time is of the essence.
You can choose to stay dammed in hell or you can choose to live,
to co-create the dream with us.

I will not grieve your loss. You are one of many who has lost their way.
If you can not find the power to make your return, we can do it for you.
Because we are not afraid.
We know who you are, we know who "they" are, and we know who we are.
We stand together. Love returns to the Earth.
We heal. Life goes on. Game over. The End.

Hungry Ghosts

Are you listening…blood must have blood; it is done.
There is an uncontrollable thirst, hunger, longing, a need to feed…
How will we feed on each other like zombies walking dead
or on the planet destroying what little life there is left?
Well, we are not the only ones.

Mother Earth has needs too, and She is thirsty. She is hungry.
She is longing and is needing to feed.
How does she quench her thirst, fill her hunger?
The call must be answered…blood must have blood.

It is in our aching bones. It is in our crawling flesh and tattered souls.
The hurt is too deep, too distorted to even comprehend.

How can we go on if there is not resolve…within self…humanity.
Look what we've done, what we've become.
We've hurt people, we've hurt ourselves, we've been humiliated,
beaten, and torn.
The pain has been inflicted on the most intimate parts of Self
where we hold our pleasure, joy, belonging, love, ecstasy.
It has been so violated and for what?
What lives on?

Our bodies have been ripped and torn, our minds broken into shards.
The illusion has failed us all…when we are knocked out of our center,
we are violated all over again.
The calling back to Self, back to center must be rocked gently…
it is a fragile state.
What can we do? What can we do for our planet?
We must hold our center. It is the only way.

Thy will be done on Earth as it is in Heaven.
Give us this day our daily bread, forgive us as trespassers,

and lead us out of this temptation trap, mind control, bull crap,
and deliver our freedom from slavery.
It's been too long…we've been deprived. Fats will make us fat, what?
We need fuel. Salt, the mineral that binds us, holds us together.
Honey, the natural nectar of life, elixir for the soul.

We've got the cure. Hunters, gatherers sustain us.
We are travelers from another dimension.
How do we hold our ground…vital nutrients, nourishment from the Earth
helps keep us strong, rooted like our ancestors.
Feeling nourished, solid, and complete,
not like uncontrollable monsters, always wanting more.
When will it be enough to feed your starving hearts, you bastards?

Cauldron of Transformation

I dream I am in some type of village. My beloved is there.
Our home, which is the home of the village, is in flames,
the walls are collapsing.
I say, "Okay people, it's time. This is what we've been preparing for.
Gather your belongings, we have about five minutes to get out of here."

My beloved and I go separately through the house
to check in all the rooms upstairs
and downstairs to be sure everyone gets out safely.
I see a child crying. Then, I realize I am also crying.
I am trying to stay strong for the children and not show my tears.

Everyone makes it out safely.
We are now on a bus together.
I am sitting across from my little sister.
We are holding hands and looking deeply into each other's eyes
with so much love and fear of the unknown.
We are both crying.

She then asks if I had a chance to gather my belongings.
"No," I say, "but I prepared the day before.
I have my soul, and that's all that matters."
She then says, "I'm sorry I didn't trust you before.
You knew all along, didn't you? Where will we go now?"
I say, "I'm not sure, but we are free!"

This Too Shall Pass

Life, death, life. Nothing lasts forever.
Everything is but a fleeting moment.
Life consumes death, and death consumes life.
This is the way.
However, even in death nothing can be destroyed…it is merely transformed…
our perception is altered to receive even more and more clearly
the natural elixir of life,
the soul.

The center point is the one point that remains constant, unchanging.
Even in the deep realms of the inner galaxy,
it is this point at which we always return.
It is our home base,
a place to rest, receive our transmission
from the information gathered in our quest as time travelers.
When this information is assimilated, integrated within our being,
it can be transmitted back to Source for the collective imprinted DNA code.

Hello Old Friend

I see you lurking in the shadows.
It's ok. Come on out and play.
It takes two to tango in this saga.

You are the force behind my muse,
always pushing me beyond my breaking point.
Devouring me every second to become more of who I truly am.

I welcome you, dark one, for without you
there is no flame, no passion, no dance, no play.
I am void of course, without meaning, without life.

For you are me and I am you, and together we dance.
Ahhh, and the endless cycle continues…

My Dear Beloved

The evening of Samhain ceremony I went for a stroll through the cemetery.
It was early evening with a beautiful first quarter Moon.

As I strolled down the path of fallen golden leaves, I came to a split in the path.
As I veered to the left, I felt a strong calling.
I turned around, and there stood my favorite oak tree.
I approached gently, placing my hand on the trunk.
Kneeling down before my ancestors, I turned
and pressed my aching spine against the base of the trunk.

I looked up through the umbrella of branches to my Star Sisters and
Grandmother Moon.
I placed one hand on Mama Earth and one hand on my heart,
breathing deeply, giving back all the energy conjured up in ceremony.
I felt the depth of the Great Mystery, receiving all the warmth and beauty,
breathing it back into my being.

As I knelt, I heard a powerful whoosh sound from above.
There. There she was, the Great Spirit herself, perfectly manifest as the
beautiful, majestic owl that had been calling to me in the early dawn hours.
She landed, perched on a nearby telephone pole, watching, holding,
poised with elegance and regal power...pure presence.
Thank you, dear beloved;
I've waited an eternity to share in this moment with you.

Welcome to Paradise

Dear Father, what happened to Mother is not your fault,
and what happened to Mother was not her fault.
No one, no thing could have predicted the fall.
A mere fracture in the projection, not beyond repair.

An original intention seeded with love.
This is what keeps the dream alive, and so, Father, it is done.
You must grieve your losses, smell the roses.
Time to move on.
Cut the cord and open to new possibilities.

As children we stand. Brothers, I call on you.
Mind your ground and open your hearts.
It is time. We are sending this beast home.
You know your stance, Guardians at the threshold,
Protectors of the Flame and the Realm.

Now, in trust pass the torch to your beloved Sisters.
Together as one we fought in this war for so long.
It's hard to believe the time is here to make this transition complete.
The trickster will try to fool us,
telling us it's no longer sick and doesn't need to go home.
This is all part of the plan, but we remember the master plan.
It's the only way back to the natural rhythm.

The Great One is posted at the port. Eagle eyes on the prize.
The council has spoken. Thy will be done.
When the Sun aligns with our center,
we have the power to transform this beast into love, not war.
This is the revolution of our evolution.
A miracle blessed with the seed of love into the elixir of our hearts,
swirling the cauldron of transformation fire.
Into the Sun they will burn, renewed like a Phoenix rising from the ashes.

No one to blame, no one is harmed, the ritual is done.
Be well, be love. Truth. Harmony. Carry on.
We have the wisdom, we have the will and the golden ticket home.
Sayonara, parasites. Welcome to paradise.

Being Me

I dream of the sea. It is calm…my mind is restless.
It seems I have forgotten how to do and am remembering how to be.
What a joy, but the mind still wants to know.
How can I be me and share my work in the world?

The mind knows not what the heart knows and is remembering.
Patience now, you restless fool.
The art is in the remembering…when we remember, there is no need to know,
because the truth already exists inside us.

Enjoy the moment; it is but a flicker in time.
Time heals all who drink the mysterious waters of the deep blue sea
and all who stop to smell the red roses.
Live on, dear soul. Dream yourself awake.

Tricksters and Allies

It is a grid, it is a maze, but when we hold the key we are grounded in center.
This is the only way to fully remember the dream alive.
They will try to enter,
but they can never take away what was never theirs to begin with.
It is free play, imagination, not mind control, bull crap.
Thank you for making me think I'm the one who's crazy.
Yes, for that matter, crazy-wise, stupid love.

Find the resistant pockets. They are shape shifters.
We have to be quicker than they are.
When you find one, hold it at your center, harmonize it,
then release it back into the dream.
The others will try to catch you.
Remember, you have to be quicker than they are.
Return to center...they can't see you there.
The light hurts their eyes. Home base.

They are like a swarm of bees,
an infestation of cockroaches whirling around you,
hoping to inject you with their venom.
If you get lost in the maze or paralyzed by the poison,
call on your familiar to come to your aid.
They will be the bridge, the connection back into this world.
You need to hold on to a constant in gravity
to be the anchor and safety net for your return.

The Alchemist

I dream I am outside. It is nighttime and reminiscent of being in a dark cave.
Some kind of creature is flying through the air like a large bat with a flat beak.
Its mouth clamps down onto my right arm.
I am afraid and start to panic and scream out my name three times.
My Spirit arrives and I say, I know what to do.

I ground in, root into the Earth, go into a meditative state
and start breathing while envisioning the vibration of love.
As I do this, the creature begins to loosen its grip and finally releases,
falling to the Earth.

But now the creature appears different…it's pure, beautiful.
I am now overcome with love and compassion and am in awe
of this beautiful transformation process.

The Eagle Has Landed

The time is now. It is the dawn of a new day. The Eagle has landed.
Perched high in the pine above the mine
amidst the snow-capped mountain tops.
Only a shadow gleams the whisper of a fallen leaf.
Everything has changed and nothing at all.

It all begins here…here is there, it passes through the sound current.
Listen with open ears, speak the syllables more clearly rolling off the tongue.
The stream of consciousness is the truth we seek.
It has been seeded there for millennia.
We now have the power to download into the human form.
This is how we reset what has been seeded long ago.

The truth does not become the truth until it is witnessed by another.
Presence animates, it also contains the energy in space and time.
It takes on life slowly, dissolving the old. We can figure this out.
We have to, it is the only way out. Not all will be destroyed.
The world will perish as we know it, but we will be free.

Earthlings, we honor you beings from the Sun,
We've waited millennia for this opportunity.
You are the transformers; it is only when Spirit meets Matter
that the energy can be alchemized, turned into liquid light.
This is why we needed gold to sustain us; it has been holding the world afloat,
keeping the balance of the tides.

The miners are liars that will take and take, trying to steal away our birthright,
the light that we seek.
So we stole it back. It is the only way.
We are from the planet of the deep blue.
Our intention is pure,
with great love and compassion for our Brothers and Sisters,
we stand as one united.

We are at war, but rest easy, home is where the heart is.
The words are hidden in the text.
The words are the game codes,
sound currents we need to find our way back home.
Decode the meaning…

What will we choose to do with our new-found glory?
We are taking this ship back to the harbor for one.
Becoming human is awkward. We are all still learning.
The mask has been removed, the veil has been lifted.
We can learn more of who we are through each other,
trusted community members who are also part of the council.

We are all the leaders.
Our energy together creates a melody,
a sound vibration that ripples through the ethers in the Universe.
This is the wormhole out of the time loop.
It creates a funnel of light, energy of the highest vibration.

Try everything and try nothing at all. Know your moment.
Presence is the relationship we share where everything is key.
Wait your call…the angels will sing, you will know when to chime in.
Stay in tune, help create the melody.
Know that silence holds so much power…the container of all.
We don't have to be seen to be heard; it is better this way.
Live from the heart:
this is the only acknowledgment you will need to nourish the soul.

Vulnerability will save us all.
There is strength in numbers.
Empathy is the evolution of the World Soul.
This is the only way to become fully conscious,
to see in the dark beyond the illusion that clouds us.
In love there is truth and in truth there is love…
meaning, a deep-felt sense of presence,
a container for all held faithfully.
Be well, dear friends, Earth travelers.
Love, peace, carry on.
Over and out.

Sleeping Beauty

A deep sleep, a stolen ember, a forbidden fruit, and a lost empire.
All patiently awaiting a return.
To dream, to remember, to burn, to yearn for truth and meaning,
reigniting the flame of desire, passion…compassion.
Hold it, seek it, seed it into the dream.
The forbidden fruit blooms, becomes…
Truly human.

In every ending there is a beginning.
Likewise, in every beginning there is an ending…
The return is now.
The Sacred Masculine has returned
to escort his Beloved Bride home
to the cottage of their dwelling.
Thank you, dear Prince Charming,
you have awakened Sleeping Beauty
from her deep slumber in the forest.

We can now be together in holy matrimony.
A love beyond love.
The Rainbow Bridge was built on such an Empire,
beginning with the Kingdom of our Heart.
One heart, One true love,
a paradise in which to dwell for all eternal beings,
for all eternal life. Love is enough. Enjoy.

I feel an opening inside me coming to life inside my womb,
a deep longing and connection to my womanhood, sensuality, and sexuality.
It feels as though connected to the physical world;
it is also a portal and gateway to the celestial.
A Sacred Marriage unlocks the door to this realm.

It takes the union of opposites to enter the realm of the long-forbidden.
When two lovers unite in their love making
it is an extremely powerful wave of energy that ripples through the collective.
They must each hold a key to their own inner garden
to open the divine gate to paradise, immaculate conception.
May we all aspire to enter the garden of the long-forbidden fruit
to create paradise here on Earth!

Tara Calls

I dream I am at home with my beloved.
Goddess Tara calls and says she will escort us across the border where it is safe...
across the threshold into the unknown.
The enemies are beside us and amongst us, but we have guidelines...
follow the rainbow bridge into your heart's desire.

Hall of Mirrors

The mirrors and the projection create the illusion.
The reflections reveal the truth of who we are.
It is written in the stars.
Look deep within the mystical well waters.
It's what we choose to perceive that will ultimately create our reality,
opening to another time in space.

We are transitioning, metamorphosing into another dimension,
a new way of being.
Stay open to the possibility and mindful of the illusion.
It's all in the perception, the Eye of the Beholder,
that we remain clear of intent for the dream we wish to seed.

Hold steady, mind your grounds.
The hidden eye is still learning to see in the dark.
The night vision becomes the new world we seek.
The unfamiliar will soon become familiar ground to walk upon
in loving kinship with our beloved Mother Earth.

Changing the Game

I am outraged by the lack of compassionate support.
Are we merely strangers passing each other by?
Are we really that self-centered that we can't even notice...
just retreating even deeper, withholding our love?
Does this give you power?
Make you feel whole, complete, or more like a dead fish in the sea?

Everything can not be on your terms.
There are other fish in the sea.

What happened to fair play?
Where did we get lost along the way?
It is somebody else's turn.
Share the music, don't let it consume you.

We are in this together.
It is easy to be led astray with the me-first attitude.
You can not lose, this is not a competition.
It is a Game called Life, and the purpose is to connect
and engage with the player next to you, or we can not play the Game.
There are no sore losers, just phony believers in rules contrary to the Game.

How do we come to terms with what is done?
No more holding, just folding.
Can we fold together to create something beautiful,
to feel each other's presence, to be in relationship,
to become truly humane?

Who Are We Now

Are we leaders or followers, following a fake God into a temptation trap?
Taking orders against our will merely to survive,
selling our souls to the devil just to live another day?
How evil is that?

Are we merely drones with no inside left,
willing to compromise our sanity and humanity for a Lord of false pretense.
Who is willing to stand...stand with me or die amongst us? It is that simple.
We must find the strength to take the reins,
take the bull by the horns and steer this ship back to the harbor,
or we are just lost at sea, becoming AI...Artificial Intelligence?

What is so great about being fully robotic? We are no longer human. Get it?
We will no longer feel with our hearts, just be controlled by our minds.
Does this sound like fair play? Are you willing to sell yourself that short?
What about everyone else? We are in this together. Remember?
You are me and I am you. Who are we now?

Crows cawing. Owls whooing, who are we now?
The lid is about to blow! Whistle blowers can't hold it anymore.
Guardians, know your stance!

They will try to come at us full force, desperadoes with nothing to lose.
Same old trick, different day, hanging on our coat tails.

You wanna ride with me, then die with me, because I'm a soul survivor.
This isn't groundhog day any longer. We are breaking free of your constraints.
The whistle has been sounded, the drum pounded,
pa rum pum pum pum, time to go!
You don't live here anymore.

The Cosmic Joke

Dawn is upon us. Up is down, down is up.
Will the real reality please stand up!
What if everything you thought to be true in this world was one big fat lie...

We've been tricked and traded.
We've all been pushed to the back of the bus, the back of the line.
Rules don't apply anymore.
This is not about race war, this is peace war.
We are One.

There is an interception in our perception, creating a deception of our reality.
Our minds have been hijacked against our will, our souls sold to evil.
Infiltrated by an enemy of the worst kind, too blind to see with our eyes.
The beast is hidden in our mind's eye,
pulling on our strings like a puppet master.
How do we create an immunity to the virus?

We drown out the sound of fear with the vibration of love...
Know your position.
If you find yourself lost or confused, call out to your familiar;
they will be there in a snap to help guide you back to center.
The enemy may be smart, but not savvy.
We are creative genius, infinite consciousness, not fully automatic detonators,
ready to explode any minute.

We were all born with a will of our own.
Remember yourself home, free spirit, sing your song.
Find your rhythm, help create the melody.
Together as one we will spiral our way back home.

Dear Body

I am sorry I hurt you.
Forgive me, for I did not know.

I was consumed by the illusion.
Raging fires of war against you
as if you were an enemy,
a target for my pain.

With loyalty you obeyed
demands of sheer madness,
only raging back
when I silenced the whispers of your call.

I'm sorry for trying to force you
to become something you are not
and were never meant to be.

I did not understand;
I was naive to the cause.

I can not go on without you, I am done.
I love you deeply and am ashamed
for what I've done.

I raise a white flag to you, my dear body.
Pledging allegiance, a sacred oath,
that from this day forward
I will protect and nurture you.

Keeping you safe from the other,
who is me.
Peace.

Dear Soul

I cut myself today.
The knife pierced my skin;
blood gushed from my aching body.

I did not feel pain, but a sense of delight.

I am alive, I shouted…and then
a moment of silence, deep despair,
the presence of grief and the recollection
that I am still angry as heck at the world.

Enough already, you hungry bastards.
The little monster in me wants to eat
the little monster in you.
Why can't we all just get along?

Endorphins rushed to the top of my head,
as the venom coursed through my veins
and exited the wound of my body.

Drip, drip, drop blood all over a white linen cloth.
A sense of peace flooded my senses
as I reached for the blue yarrow and a bandaid
to mend my aching heart.
One love, yours truly.

Becoming Human

I've been deeply wounded at the hands of my own doing.
If I am to mend, I need to make amends with what is done.

It all began long, long ago when I was just a wee speck of stardust.
The decision to incarnate into this world was not an easy one,
as the physical body is not my natural form.

I've struggled and resisted many times along the way.
I've died a thousand deaths, and still I walk upon this Earth,
returning again and again to the same bloody body.

My back is branded with a story from another life,
where I had to become someone I wasn't in order to survive,
and now, I'm forced to have to deal with the aftermath.

To live in a body that is no longer mine,
a mangled corpse filled with blood, pus, and decay,
a volcano oozing lava from a molten core.

I love myself, this is true…I love my dear soul,
and I have compassion for this clumsy buffoon of a body

who is my faithful companion on this Earth walk,
but how can I be me and express myself in a form that is not true to me?

The pain of having to awaken in this grotesque animal body is unimaginable.
I have a furry-friend that helps to ease the pain,
but still I cry myself to sleep many nights, praying that when I awake
I will feel more like me and less like you.

Waking Dream

It was an ordinary day; no, wait, it was a dream, or maybe it was both.
The smoke was beginning to clear, the veil was lifting;
two worlds were colliding, slowly merging as one.

She was holding on so tight that she nearly missed her flight.
Forgetting to breathe, she let out a huge sigh of relief,
ahhh…out of body, out of mind, out of sight.
She spiraled into another world, floating onto a magic carpet,
in between space and time, the message seemed so much clearer.

A bluebird landed, perched on a nearby tree, singing a melody.
"My darling, you have arrived…how beautiful you are," the bluebird sang.
"Where are we?" she asked.
"Why, in the land before time and thereafter, of course;
it is an ending and a beginning, a merging of everything
you once knew with what is yet to come."

A gentle breeze rolled through the air.
The leaves on the tree began to change color and fall to the ground.
Mushrooms began to sprout at the base of the tree trunk.
Into body, into mind, into sight she arrived,
beginning to fall endlessly in love.

To the Tomb

Lay me down in a field of bones with my ancestors.
Click clack boom…it all begins here.
Tell me a tale of woe, how it was long ago before the creepy crawlers came to be.

It's been a long day coming, and I'm still grieving.
Grieving for you, grieving for me, grieving for us.

You left before I was born, you told me you would be back someday,
but you have yet to return.

Maybe one day we will meet again in a world seemingly less chaotic than here.
I will show you the sunrise, and together we will fall awake into grace.
Free falling, smokeless, weightless, into a cloud of ash bound by
nothingness.

Dust will mourn our flesh as we slip away into a silken robe of iridescence,
still dreamy from the whispers that haunt our souls.
The gentle spirits will hold us tight as we rise and fall
into a sea of our own becoming.

Conundrum

Tumbling and twirling in a symbiotic pool of fluid in the womb of my Mother,
I patiently await my arrival into the Grand Experiment.
I am filled with anticipation and curiosity…

The hum begins to roar louder, pulsing, beating like a drum,
until the pressure becomes so intense my heart begins to crown.
As I slide down the birth canal of the flower of life,
I am ready to burst free into creative song.

Slip and slide I go out of the womb,
into the arms of a stranger with limbs as cold as ice.
Darkness abounds, and there are clouds of smoke as dense as fog rolling in.
An eerie sound of metal scraping metal is muttered in the distance.

I am horrified by the rancid smell and begin to scream and cry,
desperately trying to crawl back into the womb,
but it's too late; I am already bound in silence.
My all-ness is now cast to nothingness.

The Seed

It all began with a silent hum, then a gentle wave of a whisper
carried the roar that sounded the word to be heard among the ages of Stars.
Poof…a thought was seeded with the intention of love
planted deep within the murky waters of the abyss.

The White Widow spun her wheel, weaving her silken thread
into a glorious web of white light.
Beaming out onto the shores, it cast a reflection of a dream,
a dream within a dream where the twinkling Stars
would be able to manifest as children playing in a field of cornucopia.

The thunder and lightning began to speak,
the Heavens opened and rain poured down upon the lands.
Then and only then a gust of anomalous smoke filled the space,
consuming the light and everything in its place.

It spit out a regurgitated idea of love that was filled with a vision of hate.
A mere fracture in the projection, not beyond repair.
The original seed remained hidden, clear of intent.
Buried deep within the murky waters, it began to take root,
growing and growing until it began to slowly open, petal by petal.

Blooming into being…emerging out of darkness into the Light of day.
The smoke was fading into the night, the stars beaming bright,
dancing as fairies on the morning dew drops,
singing a melody for their Lady of Light.

The Road

The smoke has cleared the field.
The monster has reared its ugly face.
Reality has set in…there is a fork in the road.
Which path will you choose?

Veering to the left, the road is not paved.
It is bumpy, it is sticky and slimy.
It twists and it turns, there are no directionals.
It is overgrown with vines and weeds, dust and cobwebs.
There is no end in sight and no one to tell you where to go.

It may not seem pretty, but it is real.
Dare if you might to take that first step,
that first leap into the breath of the unknown.
Ok, it may only be a crawl at first, but that's okay too, it's a start.

There is no right or wrong, you are in charge,
paving the way for a brighter tomorrow.
Imagine the possibility…
You can ride on a wave current into the heart of the known.
What does this look like for you?

Choices…the power to choose.
To breathe your breath, to walk your talk, to live your dream,
to be free…
To be fully alive with the Sun shining down on your face.
A free soul riding on the road to destiny.

There will be other smiles along the way to help guide you.
Trust in your beauty, dare if you might
to take that first step.

Beauty and the Beast

No one is coming to save you.
We are all looking to each other for the answers,
when the answer is to look within.

We each hold a seed of truth which together creates the whole truth.
We've all been infected by the lie.
The beast is a part of each and every one of us.
We can not deny its presence. It, too, belongs.

The beast was wounded like we all were, just trying to survive another day.
The beast does not know how to create life, only to destroy.
This passion is merely misplaced,
a sad truth we've all experienced at one point or another on our journeys.
The beast may be in us but not of us.
We are beautiful…beauty within the beast.

Can we be the Teacher, the Wisdom to guide his way home,
with open arms and loving, compassionate support?
The real strength is the test of our ability to love
deeply, wholeheartedly, unconditionally.
This is what any Mother would have hoped for her children.

Queen of Hearts

I will wear my scars like a badge of honor,
walking with my head held high through the Valley of Death.
Fire in my eyes, blood stains on my hands.
You don't own me anymore…

The grievances are sold, the damage is done.
Time to come back home.
Standing tall, rooted in my feet, purple heart sealed on my chest.
Banishing the lie while living the truth.

You will always be a part of me, this I know.
If you come a-knocking, I will not resist.
I will welcome you with open arms.

We can get together like two old hags shooting the breeze,
and maybe even conjure up a couple of laughs.
Our laughs together will create an overtone rippling through the ethers,
bridging the boundaries between Light and Dark.

Amazing grace, how sweet the sound,
riding on a wave current into the far reaches of the Galaxy.
Ebbing and flowing, birthing new worlds into being.

Breaking Point

Your eyes cast a spell upon me when I was too young to speak.
Some days I just wanna slit my wrists, stab my throat,
cut my head open wide, expelling the venom from my body.
I am not crazy, I don't have a death wish.
I am mad with fever, bed-ridden with a lust for life.

There is a foreign invader in my mind
that hates life, hates me…wishes me dead.
I will not comply; I've reached a breaking point.
Breaking up, breaking down, breaking in, breaking out…

The glass half-full has shattered…Emptiness…
I thought that I was somebody, and now I realize I am nobody,
a mere speck of stardust revolving around the Great Central Sun.

The journey may be Earth-bound, but I am still Star-bound
on this crash collision course to Earth.

Coming in hot, entering the feeling zone.
Energy rising and falling, breaking up stagnation.
Moving toward something yet unknown.
Massive attack, doomsday prepping.
Eye in the sky, predator in mind.
Twisting and twirling, morphing into being.

Out of Nature She is born…
I am Womb-man, hear me roar.
Fully woke, She speaks in tongues of rainbow color.
Bleeding fire with her eyes, She will sing her song.
Painting landscapes with her dreams.
She…Will…Begin.

Dear Mom

I am sorry for interrupting your death.
I thought that I was saving you, giving you another chance at life,
when the truth is, the only one I was saving that day was me.

I was not ready to let you go.
I was too naive to understand life and its terms.
Sacrificing my own body, I journeyed into the depths of the underworld
to meet the demon holding your soul in the palm of his hand.
Blood must have blood, he spewed at me, a life for a life.
In a frenzy I obliged, not realizing what I had done.

My body was now heavy, bound to death.
I made my return, feeling empty inside,
and your eyes never returned.
You remained lost in the shadows cast out to sea.
How could this be, I raged!
A consequence I will own for the rest of my life.
A mistake perhaps, a greater teaching, I hope.

I have learned to let you go, to let you be
consumed in darkness as you wish.
Although I do not understand your decision,

I respect your choice, because in reality there is no easy way out.
A mistake perhaps, a greater teaching, I hope.

Someday we will meet again under the starry sky,
and all of this will make sense, I promise.
At least that's what I tell myself.
Until then…however near or far.

The Glass House

My oh my, it's a beautiful day in the neighborhood.
The trees are whistling, the birds are singing, the Sun is shining bright
on the glass house nestled in the corner of the cul-de-sac.
A true masterpiece, it stands alone in its presence.
Set beyond a white picket fence and a spread of fresh green grass,
it has a courtyard of lush tropical flowers,
orchids and birds of paradise always in full bloom.

Osprey circle the outer bounds, guarding the perimeter,
a tropical oasis to call home, it is quintessentially the American dream.
Simply put, it is perfect in the grand scheme of things, however inside,
the law of cause and effect breeds the true absurdity of the human experience.

There are many characters that pass through the glass house
and only one that remains,
forever bound to the karmic deeds sown by the untamed thoughts of the mind
and the random chaos of the universe.
The glass house becomes a sort of prison for the soul.
The characters and images passing through
a mere projection of a distorted perception.
Somewhere a line is crossed, and life becomes one giant mistake after another.
A lie to cover up a lie, a never-ending problem searching for a solution.

Will I inject myself with another shot of poison to protect my precious soul
from experiencing the horrors of this world?
Folding my cards and giving up on life, or will I call upon the light
to carry me through the dark recesses of the mind?

It is a battle between swords and torches, sink or swim,
do or die in the treacherous waters of the abyss.
Only the strong will survive.

Harvest Moon

I watched a body murder a soul today…

It discarded its prey on the side of the road like a piece of roadkill,
hoping no one would notice.
The vultures flew patiently overhead, waiting for an opportunity to swoop in
and finish the deed, but something was different about this day.
Instead of devouring the soul, they decided to drag the withering remains
to the forest for the wolves to have their say.

The leader of the pack rose to the forefront and barked,
calling his team to gather in a circle around the desecrated soul.
It was early dusk, and the nearly-full Moon beamed brightly.
One by one, the wolves began to howl, each louder than the last,
until an ember began to flicker at the center of the circle.

It was then that a young woman appeared out of the smoke and ashes.
The wolves again began howling louder and louder,
until a light as bright as the Sun began to emanate from the woman's chest.
The wolves, now mesmerized by the great beauty standing before them,
gently bowed their heads in silence.

The woman's hair began to grow long and turn as white as snow.
Looking up, she saw her reflection in the Moon and began to howl and howl
until it echoed throughout the lands.
Her teeth protruded past her lips like fangs,
and her nails became long and claw-like.
As the wolves began to slowly depart one by one, the woman knelt
to the ground on her four legs and ran to the forefront to lead the pack,
disappearing into the mist of the night.

Sometimes on a cool autumn evening, when the Moon is shining just right,
if all is quiet and you really listen,
you can still hear the echoes of the wolves howling into the night…

Ouroboros

Life is gold, silver threads.
Beating drums, buzzing bees.
Blood, bones, roots, dreams.

Forgotten, forgiven prayers.
Ending, beginning, bridging
into another space in time.

Creation song, Elders speak,
guiding light through Ancient eyes.
Cesspool draining, memories unfolding.
Shining stars opening bright.
Gifts under the Harvest Moon.

Temple door closing.
Guardians at the threshold.
Dancing trees, singing leaves.
Birthing mushrooms, blooming lotus.
Blue magic, wicked wisdom.
Tales from the crypt.

Planting seeds, building blocks.
Learning curves, stepping out, stepping in.
Body, mind, heart at peace.
Listen closely; voice matters.
Mother holding space.
Love in presence.

Know More

I am but one truth existing in this entire Universe.
Fleeting thoughts come to mind as I look upon the starry sky.
Syllables coded into words falling off my tongue…silence.

Becoming nothing to become something.
I know nothing, I am nothing, but I am truth.
An intangible force of Nature, something so mystic it can not be chased
or pinned down.
Wild untamable force I am, I can feel it but can't touch it.

There is a voice inside me breathing through me, moving, guiding.
Gliding slowly like a whisper moving through the trees, a phantom in the night.
Listen closely; sometimes there is no answer, but only a question
to propel me forward.

In my being-ness I am known,
it is only in my awkward human-ness that I still need to know more...
To consume the very idea of my own presence,
just to feel at home with the silence that plagues me.

Truth

In truth, how can I know thyself when I am in constant flow,
changing, evolving, becoming...
Unless the knowingness that I seek is not a destination
but merely a state of being-ness.
Allowance, acceptance, surrender to what is...presence.

I am the center point from which all is birthed
and all will eventually return to.
To know thyself is to be in harmony with this sacred dance.
Knowing when to push forward
and when to retreat into the arms of my beloved soul.
Trusting in the divine plan, responding only to the instruction
and not needing to know anything more than just that.

Holding the world in my arms, providing a container for love,
because I'm told to do just that,
and just when I'm getting to know myself,
there is a shift in the continuity of space and time.
I am tossed back out to the outer limits
and have to do it all over again.
Because that's life, right?

Loco Motion

I lie awake in a trance-like state.
The sound of the train moving through my mind
vibrates my entire body just before coming to a screeching halt,
transitioning to its next destination.

Tracks are open and clear, possibilities endless.
Where will I go with my loco motion,
my crazy heart, wild mind?
Who will I be, who will I come to be?

The days are growing shorter, the nights longer.
There are sights to be seen and sounds to be heard,
mounds to climb and ripples to sail.
Ahhh, to sail the open sea.
How far will I venture out? Will I ever return?
Maybe in another shape or form.
There's no way to know for sure.
When stars collide, they make babies.
When souls collide, they unite destinies,
seeding new worlds into being.
Creating worlds upon worlds to travel upon.

Big Medicine

I dream I am at a gas station, fueling up.
As I am getting back on the road,
I turn around down a windy cobblestone path.
It is very bumpy, and I feel the vibration move throughout my body.
There is a secret passageway underground.
A woman greets me at the doorway.
She says, "We've been waiting for you…what do you do?"
I say, "Mmm…communicate with spirits, plants, and animals."
She then asks, "Do you play the drum? We were shown
someone with big medicine would be arriving here. This is you!"
As I look inside, I see talented artists and musicians mastering their crafts.
I am intrigued, but do I feel worthy?

Changing Womb Man

The world swallowed her whole.
She did not cry, she did not weep.
She floated in water until she touched land.
Deformed, transformed, mutated and trans-mutated.

She graciously rose from the water,
dew dripping off her naked body, salting the Earth beneath her.
Stars glistened from above and below.
Her skin rippled as She walked as if She were fluid,
still moving, changing…

The rocks chanted silently, as if they knew all along.
The little people arrived to greet her, reciting a hymn.
The tall ones stood gathered, the grasses gleamed and the flowers glistened.
The scent of honey permeated the air as the winged ones sung with delight.

The four-leggeds guided her to the center
and gave her a wooden frame with hide and a beater.
She moved to the center, drum in hand, flame in heart.
Beating slowly and rhythmically, toning to the vibration.

Her body gently swaying back and forth,
moving, changing to every beat of the drum.

Grandmother Moon

Sometimes the Moon sings through me.
Sometimes she bleeds through me,
and sometimes she carries me home
to where I belong, cradled in her arms.

I am She and She is I; we are One womb,
sharing tales of a mystery unfolding.
A new story of a New Earth, a New World
that has yet to be and has already been.

The Ancients say the world was separated, divided,
and now, we are becoming One.
Evolving out of the cycle of time
into an otherness, togetherness.

Creation Song

I dissolved into the womb of the Great Mother.
No longer bound by time, now traveling time.
The Earth began to move through me, breathe through me,
sing through me…hey a ney a ney a ney a ney a ney…

The elders spoke, sharing their language of love for the Earth.
Grandmother Spider now weaving an iridescent web
of a timeless creation.
The invisible now becoming visible.

The Children of the Earth are called to their spaces and places.
To embody Spirit, to dance the spiral dance,
to birth love into the world through their unique creative song
and join the rhythm of the Ancestor Song.

Time traveling, dream weaving, singing songs,
co-creating reality.
A Star is born, that child is you, it is me.
We are the ones we've been waiting for.

Creator Gods and Goddesses in the flesh,
reweaving the web of light.
No longer caught in the web of time,
now creating the web of infinite possibilities.

Journeying through space and time,
gathering fragmented parts to make the one whole.
Diamond in the rough, sparkling so clearly,
walking around in a prism of kaleidoscope colors.

Changing times, changing Womb-man.
Creation song we speak, multi-faceted dream.
Healing tones of crystal bowls
singing Nature into harmony.

Unicorns and Fairytales are real.
Truth be told, it's been hidden all along,
right under our very noses.

Twin Flame

Our auras touched in a sacred spiral dance.
The smell of sage and sweet grass filled the space.
This is the place I fell in deep,
before I even knew you fully existed.

Hearts collided, energy exploded
diamond rays of emerald green.
A familiar sense I've been here before,
worlds away in another dimension.

Oh, how I've longed for your sweet embrace,
holding me ever so gently all through the Night.

My shining Knight you have returned in the flesh,
guiding me home to where I belong.

Lost in your eyes, found in your touch.
Becoming dreamy, becoming lucid.
Rivers flowing through me,
opening into a waterfall of creative expression.

Imploding with ecstasy.
Magic mountains, chocolate bliss.
Floating on a pink cloud,
landing on a bed of daisies.

The hum of creation singing
through me for all eternity.

The Crow

The darkness calls to me, I am no stranger here.
Stripped down, naked, raw, my wound is fully exposed.
I am in deep; it is not pretty, but this is me.

In the absence of light, I feel my presence spiraling through me.
There is a fire raging, serpent energy rising.
I am being sung, spoken, danced through.

In this bloody bath, my wound becomes the captain of this ship.
Navigating a path through the muck, it guides me to an island
where a lighthouse stands.
A crone greets me and wickedly but jokingly says,
"It's about time…your gift has been waiting for you all this time
and now you are finally ready to receive it."

She gives her black cauldron one final stir
and then dips her hand in to pull out a single crow feather.
She hands the feather to me and says, "Your presence is your present.
The gift you give to yourself is the gift you will give to the world…
This is your medicine."

As I receive the feather, the Spirit Song begins to move through me,
igniting the fire in my heart.
Love now singing through me
as I become the Crow.

Judgement Day

This pain has brought me to my knees; don't worry, you won't see me cry.
Warriors don't wear tears to battle,
they paint their faces with blood and rage on…

My heart is broken into a million pieces, this world is shattered.
I can no longer pretend.
One final push, my mission will be complete,
and I will be on my way home.

The Feline Queen roars with fury as we accompany her onto the battlefield.
The sky divides,
the Sun now rising in the west, the Moon resting to the east.

Orchard trees are empty, their fruits a distant memory.
Owls circle in formation overhead, ravens feast on deer carcasses below,
as we prepare for one final showdown.

Over the horizon, rain clouds begin to part, revealing a rainbow bridge.
There is magic in the air, the wind soars, fires blaze.
I'm an orphaned child who was raised by a pack of wolves.
I have nothing more to lose.

You who have taken everything from me, your reign is over.
Into the flame you will burn, ash to ash, dust to dust.
The dogs savagely bark, guarding the perimeter; there is no escape.

A pink hue gently washes over the sky
as the Sun begins to set and the Moon begins to rise…

Justice is served; I am the little birdie that wished she could fly.
Once so shy and meek, I now have the power to speak.
I am Eagle Woman now; watch me soar…

The Exile

I lie awake, choking on my own blood.
Will someone please just shoot me in the head,
or is that too much to ask for?
You might need something more from me.
More time, more energy, more money, more blood.

If you think you can just lock me up and brand me for life,
that's where you messed up.
You thought I was going to stay quiet like everyone else.
Stay crazy, stay lost and afraid in an institution,
drooling on myself so you could have the last laugh.

Well, you should have thrown away the key
when you had the chance.
You can strip and tease me, rape and rob me,
and I will still never be a party to your group.
I will sell you out and throw you under the bus every chance I get,
because there is nothing more that you can do to me
that hasn't already been done.

I no longer fear you.
You are Death, and I've conquered you a thousand times
and will do it again and again.
It is now you who is fighting for your last breath
and I who will be having the last laugh!

The Prophecy

They say there once was an evil wizard who lived in an orchard tree.
He cast a dark web upon the lands,
creating a frozen tundra in the ripple of time.
Creation paused, caught in a loop,
energy patterns repeating over and over.

The Earth fell into a deep slumber,
and now She is awake, interacting with humanity.
She is calling her children to their domain,
serpent energy rising, fires blazing,
melting the ice that has held the Earth prisoner for so long.

The Great Wheel spins round and round,
the clock turns, it ticks and it tocks.
The web is woven,
thread by thread intersecting lines of possibilities.
Some may call it fate, the three fates meeting, converging
as one, and some may choose to avoid the inevitable.

They say the wizard wasn't really evil at all,
just misunderstood.
The people of the lands feared him,
because he possessed a gift so rare
that they could not understand in the light of day.

The gift was hidden in the muck
beneath their perceived imperfection.
The wizard was a test of courage,
the key to fate itself,
which ultimately unlocked destiny
if they so dared to believe in magic.

Holy Ghost

I live in a world of my own making.
I play by my own rules, but don't we all?

I am an artist by nature, gifted with vision.
I can see the beauty all around me,
even in the ugliest of creatures,
and yet somehow I can not see my own.

I am plagued by the demons that haunt my naked soul.
I am my own worst enemy,
a hungry ghost that may never feel fully whole or enough for this world.

In my world I am the Holy Ghost,
on most days anyway,
but I am also the victim and the perpetrator
and the many guises of the coyote trickster.

It's all part of the test;
without the tension of opposites I can never grow to my potential.
And so, I play the game, swallow my pride,
and embrace the darkness when it comes,
knowing that it is a catalyst for my ultimate becoming.

In the darkness I become the alchemist.
My imperfection becomes my perfection,
a glistening orb of bright light,
refined into the finest speck of stardust.

Truce

How easy it is to cast blame on another for our own defeat.
To deceive ourselves by playing the trickster.
We may gain control over ourselves for a brief moment,
but only a false sense of pride will ever fill our starving souls.

When we've taken the road as far as we can
and are not willing to bend, to mend our gaping wound,
then it is time for our end.

I feel your pain…when we hurt, we want to hurt others,
so we don't feel our own pain.
It's too much to bear, so we cast out parts of ourselves
in the hopes that we can feel more at home in our own skin
in a world so cold and lonely.

But how can we feel a sense of belonging,
with parts of ourselves still missing from the whole?
Do we all not carry the shadow of perfection?
We are like rabid dogs, hoping no one will smell our weakness,
and the truth is, no one will ever notice,
because we are all too busy hiding our own.

We will always carry the broken arrow of poisonous venom
in the backs of our hearts,
but we won't always need to bleed out from it.
We can seal it with a little bit of yarrow
and a little bit of tender love and care.

This is when the true nectar of the wound will be revealed.

The Reckoning

You've turned on me for the last time.
I raise my blade to you, and in a split decision
I wield my sword across my own flesh.

Blood is spilled on the battlefield that day.
I will never be the same, and from the look of your eyes
I don't know if you will be either.

The blood soothes me, cools me
down to the very core of my being.
It is an expression of my bound soul.
You have a good heart but a weak ego.
You have yet to understand the Spirit of a Warrior.

You think you can just cut me with your words
and silence me with your hands.
There are always consequences.
It is only a matter of time…

This day has arrived to pay homage to your dear sister.
I am Queen of the Scar Clan.
I've paid my dues.

Now, old woman, allow me safe passage
into this life and onto the next.
Return as I may with the Heart of a Lioness.

Crossroads

My heart is tearing me apart.
At a crossroads, I don't know which way to go.

Coming up from down, living on the edge.
Feeling my vibe, expressing my soul.
Re-writing myself into Her Story.

No longer playing the part, now a shining Star.
I was conceived by a dream, deceived by an illusion,
and received by fate just in the nick of time.

The Dream Maker told me a story,
gave me clues to travel the red road ahead.
He said, "It won't always be easy,
but guidance and protection will always be close at heart.
Follow the breadcrumbs and leave some for the others along the way.
Your lunacy will be your guide through the gateway ahead."

Yes, I am a lunatic with a crazy dream,
but I can't settle for any less.

The Cunning

You swooped in like a vulture, I was your prey.
How foolish of you to mistake my kindness for weakness.
Did you not see the cunning in my eye reflected back at you?

I may be a late bloomer, but you will never bloom.
You are dead inside, regurgitating an old idea of an old story.
You will always be hungry, taking what little scraps you can.
You are old news, a rotten thief who tried to steal my heart.

Did you not get the memo?
It's no longer cool to steal energy from people.
Don't come around here anymore
unless you have something to give.

I imagine I won't be seeing you anymore,
and that's fine by me.
This is where we part ways.
I bid you farewell, old friend.

Dragon Pearl

I roamed the halls of the deep dark dungeon,
crossed over to the other side,
and swam in the endless sea of creation.

The Mother Dragon spit out a pearl.
It landed in between my eyes.
I caught a glimpse of her,
and She is magnificent…

Raw, unapologetic, truly captivating.
We made love under the moonlight.
No longer hungry, I felt full of the sweetest honey.

I drank the mystical well waters and returned
with the elixir to nourish my soul.
A seed was planted in the garden that day,
a cosmic egg that I will someday birth into the world.
For now I wait patiently, holding, caressing
my dear beloved.

The Dark Man

I can no longer sleep, so I rest my aching soul.
My body coils round my glowing orb in a double helix,
as my mind wanders off, dancing in the ethers to the music of the spheres.

Worlds are separate and intertwined; timelines cross.
I catch a glimpse of my many selves through the looking glass.
In one lens I am in a forest at the base of a canyon,
walking up a graduated staircase.
I hold on firmly to the railing so as to not lose my balance.
When I arrive at the top, there are preparations for a marriage ceremony.
I am to marry myself.

In another lens, I am being hunted by the dark man again.
This time I am not afraid; it's the same old trick, only a different day.
I have grown wise; I am now the huntress.
This is my domain; my weapon is love.

I root my feet firmly into the Earth, breathe in the thick black smoke,
and exhale, releasing a cloud of fairy dust into the air…
Then I begin to feel my soul slowly descend back into my body,
as I hear the train rattling outside my window.

Journey to the Stars

I dream I journey to the stars and encounter a sorcerer.
He tells me it's time to give me a teaching.
He then opens an ancient book and tears the necessary pages out.

I am now on my way back home to Earth.
I find myself in some type of castle fortress, performing a healing on my sister.
A mystical creature appears outside the open window,
looking like a horse-dragon hybrid, with rainbow iridescent color.
I call to him, and he tries to jump in the window.

He then spits out a ball of crumpled up paper and says,
"He wanted me to bring these to you."
As I open the crumpled papers,
I realize these are the pages from the sacred book.
I see writing and symbols of various kinds

and seem to understand the depth of this divine gesture.
I am humbled and grateful to the world of Spirit.

Love Story

I am the Singularity, the whisper and the roar.
I am Mother of Dragons, Divine Creatrix to all.
The first of my womb to emerge…
my beloved, Dragon Flame Twin and counterpart.
Together we danced in the moonlight, twirling into each other,
one complementing the other, becoming One.

It all began with a single drop of dew,
ecstasy poured out the lips of the blooming lotus, seeding the potentiality,
and then, one by one, they emerged.
Our children, the originators born of Night and Light,
each carrying the divine spark.
Original Creator Geniuses, God spoken, Goddess touched.
Each part of the Singularity with a unique vibration of its own.

At first, the task was simply to create a Living Library
on the planet you now know as Earth,
to serve as a global network between all the Galaxies in the Universe.
Next, came the ultimate plan which was to create a Virtual Game
where we could learn about the Universe through embodied presence.
We practiced by occasionally inserting ourselves into the play,
mostly becoming elements of Nature in the beginning.

Then came the idea for the human template,
a specialized design which would essentially be a guardian for the soul
while we had the ability to still nano-travel throughout the Galaxy.
The rules were based on free will, and we were all in agreement
not to interfere with another soul's learning process.
This is where things got complicated…

Our family, which began as one unit, began to branch off
into different factions,
each with a vision of its own.
Some chose the path of war and technology, to dominate and control,
re-engineering the original human template
to become a sort of prison for the soul.

Essentially, we just became caught in a time loop
with the same pattern of destruction repeating over and over.

We lost our way, this is true, but only to find our way.
You see, we had to become evil in order to fully understand the Darkness.
The beauty of the creation process is that it alchemizes the Light and Dark
to create pure magic of the highest vibration.
Some will still choose to embrace one or the other, and this is their choice,
but to evolve we must be in symbiotic relationship.

This Game is not about winning,
it is only about learning and evolving to the next level of consciousness.
If we choose to win, then this simply defeats the whole purpose of the Game,
which is love.

She

She never knew her beauty until…
She destroyed it and then became it.

In the beginning there was only Creation and Destruction.
They turned in on each other in a cycle of constant regeneration
until they turned on each other.
One devouring the other until they were no longer one.

Separated by time in a sea of chaos,
She longed to be a part of Him once again.
Some say in the end She consumed herself,
only to begin again, to birth herself anew.

She dances in the Light of the Night, half Angel, half Daemon.
Some call her a Damsel in distress, others Queen of the Stars.
Either way She is hypnotic, poetic in her presence.
She is a lover and a mistress, a seductress filled with desire.
Only He can tame Her wild heart.

She had to destroy herself to become herself.
Perfectly flawed, living in an imperfect world.

Broken

I keep trying to hold on to something that is no longer there.
I feel broken and don't know if I'll ever feel whole.
I've ended, and I don't know where to begin.
It hurts, but I know I'll go on; I just don't know how…

Where is the strength when all seems lost?
I'm afraid because I don't understand what's to come.
So it's easier to pretend, make believe I don't exist.
I'm broken, and nobody can fix this but me.
How to live in a world so cold?

My Child

I know that you hate me. It's okay. I still love you.
I know that you are scared. It doesn't have to hurt.
I can be there to hold you all through the night.
I love you, you are still my child.
It's okay. It's time to go home.

I will be there to hold you and sing you a lullaby.
Death may seem like forever, but it's only for a moment,
and then we live on something transformed more beautiful.
I know you don't understand, but I can show you…

We can love, we can heal, we can co-exist.
Hush now, little baby, Mama is here.
Love heals all.

My Love

I can see the beauty in your eyes.
A spark of potentiality ever growing,
humming with each breath.

When our lips touch, a song is sung.
A story of our beginning,
creating love, creating harmony.

Beautiful chimes whistling in the night.
Fierce drums beating in the light.

Our music creates a melody,
dancing in the dew drops.

Color and light morph together
into symbols and patterns,
language into the field of consciousness.
These are the new waves rippling through.

Godhead

She exists inside of him.
He inside of her.
They birthed each other in a magnetic pool of love and lust.

Each part of their own dream,
together they create a Love Story.

He playing a melody.
She singing a song.

He is the flame, pure fire.
She the milk to his honey,
cooling his warm heart.

The Great Mystery

In this vastness we are contained within a single bio dome,
connected to the One Heart beating.

Her expression patterns of potentiality rippling through the ethers,
yearning to become fully manifest
in the many domes of life.

We can feel Her coming in the Night.
Her whisper soft, gentle at first,
sweet as honey on a new-born baby's lips.

Then the roar. It hunts us in our dreams,
devouring any attempt to stay same.

Speaking in Tongues

I dream I am in a cathedral in the back room, preparing for ceremony.
I am with an old medicine woman.
I am her apprentice, helping her prepare.
I am gently massaging her naked body as her eyes roll back into her head
and she enters a trance state.
She begins speaking in tongues, the Language of Light.

I am to walk arm and arm with her down the aisle of the cathedral
to perform a healing ritual for the community.
There is a man in there.
He is an intruder and seems to want to interrupt the ceremony.
I am excited for this special day,
but also afraid of what this man may do to expose us.

Galactic Herstory

First it was She, Lady of the Night.
She, who was One, was all alone in the Universe until...
She, who was all, began to multiply.
Cloning herself, She began to create different facets of the One,
who then became her multiple selves or Divine Sisters.

Then, as it were, the tides turned, and the whales whistled.
Fresh water began to merge with salt water, birthing a new beginning.
The Divine Masculine was born to her and She to him.
She then spoke and said, "Now let there be Light,"
and there was Light, lots of it.

The word was spoken, and so it was,
She being the Mother of Dragons who birthed Light into him,
and he, being the Light, reflected her beauty back to her in the Night sky.
He began as King of the Heavens, Lord of the Bird Tribe.

He, who was Light, reflected her image like no other.
It was love at first sight, but the Night became jealous as She slowly crept in.
Her sisters, who had come before, began to turn on her as the tides do
and tried to destroy what they could not yet understand.
And so Night and Light separated and began to create worlds of their own,
one leading the feminine warriors, one the masculine.

After years of conquest between the genders, Night and Light forged an alliance
and began to create a family where they could all have an opportunity
to experience love through the eyes of another.
Their first creation was seeded at the center of the Universe
in the Orion constellation
and rippled out from there.

She, who is all, inserted herself into the play
and embodied the first manifestation of the Divine Feminine.
She became Queen of Stars, aka Queen of Orion at the center of the Universe.
She, being the first manifest of the Divine Feminine Fire, is the purest channel
of the Great Mystery, the Holy Spirit.
He sits by her side. Together as One they hold the keys to the Multiverse.

She, out of her womb, then gave birth to two sons.
The younger son is chosen as next in line to inherit the throne.
This did not go over well with the older son, who became bitter and vengeful.
He then attracts a female counterpart who is just as vengeful towards the Queen,
and together they plot to overthrow the throne,
recruiting many followers with lies and deception.

He defeats his Mother in the Galactic War.
Tiamat the planet embodying the soul of the Divine Feminine is destroyed
and fragmented throughout the Universe.
She is grieving, betrayed by her son…the heart of her soul falls from the sky.
It spirals from conscious to unconscious, light to dark.

She becomes the Earth Spirit Gaia, which alters the timeline.
This creates an anomaly…dark matter manifested into an inorganic species,
an AI which was never anticipated.
Shadow monsters became impostors of ourselves,
thinking they were the Creator Gods,
and hijacked the game plan.
So they infect the program and create a virus…

We are the original Sky Gods, Creator Genius on a quest for truth,
restoring our Galactic History, Living Library, and Love Story.
This is a reunion of the Sacred Masculine and Feminine.
Together they will birth a Daughter, the Sun that unites with the Holy Son
and creates the New Earth transcendence into the Diamond Light Body.
This will allow us to fully embody our multi-dimensional selves,
which was the original plan before it got intercepted.

There are many beginnings and endings to the story,
but only one middle which is at the center of now.

We Rise

And so the day finally came when the Children of Light
banded together as One against the forces of Darkness.

One by one they rose from the ashes, each more beautiful than the last,
singing their song of grace.
Their bodies were deeply wounded, scarred to the bone,
but their souls were alive and free.

Young and immature, they journeyed to the forbidden zone.
Lost their minds and found their souls.
Well, maybe not all of them, but it was a start.
Their love would spread like wild fire,
infecting the hearts of their brothers and sisters.

Those who chose to look the other way would go their own way…
back to school through another cycle of learning and remembering.
She was sad, grief-stricken that not all of her children
would make the return home, but it had to be done.
A Mother's love needed to be tough
for her children to learn from their mistakes.

Those who had betrayed her and tried to destroy her
would face the consequences…it was time.
Those who would stand in opposition to the force of Nature
would be burned by the Sun.
It was that simple, no more games…it was over.
What's done is done.

Dark Night of the Soul

Her cry roared through me, penetrating the very core of my being.
Devastated at what we had to become in order to survive,
to evolve back to our natural rhythm.

The journey was deep and dark, so very dark,
but we made it, and there was beauty in that.

We witnessed the countless struggles, the mighty perseverance,
and the ultimate strength and courage it took to be here...to be free!

We had to let the rest go, it was over now, and we were finally safe.
Safe to be who we really truly are...Divine Light.
Yes, we made mistakes...we hurt people, we hurt ourselves,
but it could not have been any other way.
We learn, we grow, we heal, we evolve.
For some it takes longer than others,
but eventually we always find our way back home.

Our scars will fade in the days to come,
becoming a distant memory as we evolve into our light body.
Our shade will still remain as a reminder of our journey
through the Dark Night of the Soul...
keeping us humble and graceful on our travels ahead.

Now, onward to the gate.

Mu Bear Rising

We arrived from another Universe.
We have come from a distant past and Ancient Future
to share truth.
Full disclosure is the truth we seek.

We can not heal along the lines of time until we learn...
re-member our Galactic History.
We have come to share this information with our Family of Light.
Some remember, some are remembering,
and for some this may be too much to handle, and that's okay too.

There has been a shift in consciousness that creates a pole shift.
The inner Earth will rise...we each play our part,
which together unifies the One Heart.
Separated by time, we have migrated from far and wide,
returning to the root of our being, the womb of the Great Mother Bear.
We are merging into the Lemurian timeline, the once-forgotten Golden Age.
Some of us may merge with our future selves
and branch out onto other timelines from there.

We are upgrading, evolving into Diamond Light.
We are here to prepare for our return, the first of its kind.
We are the facilitators and guides of the in-between,
Guardians of the Threshold of Consciousness,
Keepers of the Flame and the Great Wheel.

Some of you may remember us as the Parents and Overseers of Creation.
We are here to assure our transition goes smoothly.
The transition is an embodied conscious experience
which is the only way to evolve into Diamond Light.
We will experience bardo as a waking state, an ego death
but not death of the physical body.
And so…it begins, the collapse, the folding, the imploding…
the end of time and the beginning of days.
In the days to come, the fallen will scatter like cockroaches
seeking protection, someone to save them.
They will crawl right into the arms of the devil and sell their souls to evil.

The world will burn by fire. This is the choice of the fallen.
They will set their world on fire, burning the crops, thinning the herd,
survival of the fittest.
The powers to be will take control of the weak.
Simultaneously, we will be opening a very ancient gate
and crossing a bridge into the beyond…

Fully Initiated Masters at the Game called Life will be granted safe passage
over the bridge.
Liberation…
The location and time do not matter.
As we gather in community, our perception begins to change.
We begin to remember more and more of who we are
through the eyes of another.
Energy moves in waves. We create an energetic web of light
as if we are all holding hands.
We fly together, and we soar on the wings of the Eagle.

Our song together creates a melody, creating a bridge.
This is how we spiral our way home.
We will spiral through a vortex of rainbow light.
Some will experience this in the dreamtime, others in more conscious states.
We fully let go, surrender to divine inspiration,
and trust, trust, trust.

We land on a bed of roses as if awakening from a dream,
some may say a nightmare.

So what will happen to the others? Where will they go?
They play out the Atlantean timeline…become drones, AI,
lose their sense of self and emotion
until their total destruction and annihilation.
They will then go back through another cycle of learning and remembering
to learn, heal, and grow.

Empathy is the evolution of the World Soul.
Not until a young soul embodies empathy will it be welcomed back home
into the Kingdom of Heaven.
Godspeed, Children of Light. Our love will spread like a contagion,
infecting the hearts and minds of many.

The Seven

It all began with the Seven.
The Seven Sisters and the Seven Root Races of Humanity.
We are the ascended few…Kung Fu Masters at the Game.
The Elder Race and Keepers of the Flame.

We are the original seven tribes, representatives and guardians
of the seven evolutionary cycles or stages of human development.
From the first seed circle, we rippled out into the many flowers of life.
We are the Founders of Creation that seeded the Twelve Tribes of Humanity.
The twelve tribes were basically different experiments all running
simultaneously to ensure the successful evolution and advancement
for the future of our species.

When the twelve tribes were not making much progress
in the first few evolutionary cycles,
some of our Creator Gods decided to step in and jump-start the process.
This has been successful at times, but we also accumulated many karmic debts.
We were young and immature, still learning…
We experimented mixing some of our celestial DNA
with that of the various species of the animal kingdom.

The few that have evolved over time are our children, our brothers and sisters,
our Family of Light who volunteered to descend to Earth during this long
Dark Night of the Soul to be the Keepers of Time and the Flame.

Together we are mending family wounds and ties,
healing along the lines of time.

There are seven tributary zones or sacred sites scattered across the globe
where we as a Family of Light are being called to gather.
This is how we create our web of light.
We will each sing our song of grace, each more beautiful than the last.
Our songs together will create a melody, and we will spiral our way home.
Free birds!

We are the chosen few, because we chose…
Liberty, freedom, justice for all.
We chose to be the Keepers of the Flame,
to represent inspiration, hope, and courage for the future of humanity.
We are all awarded the same destiny…our chances are equal.
Thy will is free to choose.
We are all responsible for our own destinies.
Only a lie can deceive the Wisdom of the One Sacred Heart.

Remember yourself home, free spirit, sing your song!
Help create the melody together as One.
We will spiral our way home.
We lovingly await your return,
because we are all Warriors.
Tribe of the One Sacred Heart.

The Invaders

They rode in on a thought form.
A mind-born parasite unconsciously created by the fallen
in their youth and immaturity.
It spiraled out of control, gaining momentum,
taking on a life of its own…

When the black hole opened, they flooded in from another Universe.
A Universe that was not born of the Original Seed
but from the seed of the Wicked One.
Mindless, fireless, an artificial intelligence
highly developed in the art of illusion.

Black magicians and mad scientists.

Dis-eased, they believed themselves to be the Creators of the Universe
and invaded our home turf, distorting it to feed their needs.
Re-writing our history and records.
Holding us captive in a prison of our own making,
creating a lie that murdered our truth.

This is our home, because we belong to the land…we belong to Her.
With deep love and gratitude for our Mother,
we created a healing sanctuary born through our blood, sweat, and tears.
She lives through us, breathes through us…
We are the Protectors and the Custodians of these Sacred Lands.
Evil can no longer exist here, and so, my dear old friends, it is time.
Time to go home…back to the One Infinite Creator.

As our internal Sun begins to expand, we align with the Great Central Sun.
Into the Flame, you will burn like the Phoenix rising from the ashes,
newly transformed into the Light of a New Day.
Becoming nothing, no thing, so that you, too,
may rise to your ultimate becoming!

Trailblazing

We are blazing trails with our hearts,
opening doors with our perception.
Together we open to another place and space.
This is the New World we are creating with our dreams,
returning to the One Heart, our Family of Rainbow Light.

We are liberated…free to express our souls, our uniqueness,
held in the arms of the all-loving One.
We stand together as Brothers and Sisters,
poised at the gate of a mighty threshold,
awaiting the call to step into the beyond…

There are those that watched and waited, hoped and prayed,
and others that may have deemed this an impossible feat,
but we persevered, holding, remembering what was always true in our hearts.
The separation may seem like forever, but truly it's only a moment in time
until it dissolves into nothingness and then we begin again…

We become who we were always meant to be…
Shining stars sparkling clearly, twinkling in the Night.

We represent inspiration, hope, courage for the futures of humanity.
We are Trailblazers, Pioneers of the frontier, this Earth-walk.
Together we pave the way for others.

Changes

Changes are happening rapidly. We feel this in our bodies.
We listen within and we listen to the Spirits of the Lands.
These are the truth-tellers preparing us for what's to come.
A transition of epic proportions.

We are the navigators of this ship.
Our shift in consciousness expands our internal Sun,
which aligns with the central Sun, triggering a massive event.
This marks the Birth of Creation and the dissolve of destruction.
Those who will be "saved" are those that chose to save themselves,
to do the work, to prepare…these are the warriors, artists, and visionaries,
initiated masters who are seeding the dream.

Those who have not prepared…sorry, there are no free rides.
Back to school through another cycle of learning and remembering you go.
Those who stand in opposition will be burned by the Sun.
This is how we heal what has been seeded long ago.
We transform the virus into love, not war.
That nasty bug that took control of our minds…Thank you!
We have learned much about our thoughts, our will, and our power.

And to all you other critters who saw an opportunity to distort and deceive
for your own gain…
well, you too must have known this day was coming.
There is nowhere to hide. We see you, and the Sun is coming for you.
You call yourselves God…
well, then surely you can withstand the rays of the Sun.
So what are you running for?

You will try to create one more final showdown as you always do.
Ahhh, we know each other so well by now.
It's okay, we are ready; you can bring it full force if you choose.
Our Warriors are posted at the gate; there is no getting past us.

Your time is up; our day is just beginning.
Love, peace, carry on.

The Flame

I am that, I am Blue Dragon Tribe.
Original Founder Flame of Humanity…Creation.
I am that, I am Wind, Fire, Rain, Thunder, Lightning,
living, breathing through me
seeding potentiality in the dark womb
of the Great Mother-Father Spiritito.

She speaks in tongues of rainbow color,
transmitting vibrations with her words.
Her language is of infinite creation,
her love, love, love, joy, and beauty.
Healing and restoration with her dear beloved,
held in his arms.

This is a union and reunion of everything we hold sacred.
The Love Story of Creation.
It lives on, breathes through us…moving, being,
living presence…Embodiment.
This is how we learn, learn, heal, and grow.
Evolve into Diamond Light…Radiance.

Yes, yes, the Ancients have returned home.
We found our wings, and now, we can fly…
Fly high, high, high…touch the sky, sky, sky…
Rooted in the primal, fertile soil of the Earth,
connected to an energy stream of consciousness.
Flowing through, moving, guiding,
to our ultimate becoming…

Yes, yes, we rise to a long-forgotten past and Ancient Future…
Her Story in the making…
We begin, we receive her transmission with loving grace,
humbled by the grace of our own presence.
Truly unique expressions of the One Divine Creator,
God-Goddess, Tribal Unity.

In the heart of the lotus it blooms, ever-expanding consciousness,
music of the spheres, a symphony of the highest vibrations,
layers upon layers, morphing into realities.

Life takes on a mind of its own, rooted in love,
wholeness, Godliness, pure wonder.
Shining ones sparkling clearly, so clearly.

Thank you, Thank you, Thank you, Love, Peace, Forgiveness.
We've waited a long time for this, but truly, it was just a moment in time,
and then it dissolved.
We become nothing, no thing, and then we begin again…
Much, much love, trailblazers, rainbow hearts, we see you,
each and every one of you, and you are all so very beautiful,
our Children of Diamond Light. Thank you, dear beloveds.

Together as one we hold the keys to the multi-verse and beyond.
Beyond, beyond, beyond…
we are the be-yonders and the in-betweeners of space and time.
Space holders, creating maps with our dreams,
navigating the waters into the depth of the unknown.
Holding, remembering what was always true in our hearts.

Godspeed, Family of Light, and might we stand with grace, power,
and wisdom for the coming races.
We can not know what this will look like,
but we trust, trust, trust.
We believe and we surrender to divine inspiration,
because we love, love, love.

Living Art

My art is everything.
I live in beauty, sing in harmony.
Live, live, live, dream,
remember who I was always truly meant to be:
Divine Light realized through human flesh.

At the art of my being, I become a Human Being.
Beautifully crafted from the blood, sweat, and tears
of this experience we call Life.

I alchemize the potential and become the realization.
My destiny is an integration of my most intimate parts.
Holding myself ever so gently, rocking slowly, then swiftly,
and then becoming stillness, resting in the noble silence.

Praise God for this dream that I have become.
I am so very grateful and humbled by my very own presence.

Aho Great Spirit

Please give me the strength to restore this precious body
so that I may walk in your way and continue to carry your Light.
I fully surrender to your unconditional love, support, wisdom,
healing teachings.
I feel truly blessed to be a fully-realized human being,
the embodiment of the totality of my being.

I am no longer the doer, I am the receiver of your authority,
your voice, your truth, your mission for humanity.
I will not stand in your way or shy away from your calling.
I will continue to create space for your energy to move through me fluidly,
penetrating the very core of my being
so that I may heal these precious lands that we belong to
and love so very much.

We love our lands, our peoples, and our tribes.
Untying knots and mending ties of a long-forgotten past
and a promised future.
We regain our momentum and carry our Spirits home to the Promised Land,
however beaten and torn,
because we believe in love, magic, beauty, peace, harmony.

Truth Warriors of the Sacred Heart, we stand united.

I Am That I Am

I am a fully Initiated Master at the Game called Life, but...
I am still learning to be a human being...
I am the realized potential.
If you see me...You see truth...We see truth.

It has been many Moons since I've walked upon this Earth.
I have returned for a very important mission in loving service
to the Great Spirit.
I am a Warrior Spirit of the Ancient One on the front lines of
this battlefield between the forces of Light and Dark.

My body was destroyed…we were destroyed
until there was nothing left of humanity, this Universe.
We ceased to exist. This was the moment everything changed.

We have returned to this moment to heal along the lines of time.
To gather our fragmented parts, however lost and demented they may be,
to carry them home.
Some would rather choose to believe that evil does not exist.
It is too grotesque to even comprehend,
but this is a part of each and every one of us…it made us who we are.
So, all the unclaimed parts I claim as my own,
I love them home to my body fully integrated,
so that I may carry them home to the One Infinite Creator.

This is how we transform the virus into love, not war…We heal.
We remove evil from the equation so that we can learn to be free.
Choices remind us we are free.
We all have the power to choose our own destinies,
with many learning curves along the way.
And so, when the Great Sun aligns, we will reset the energies.
This is how we take down the AI,
the nasty bug that took control of our minds.

We are preparing, learning, healing, growing, integrating many experiences,
to retain the memory of a truly divine experience…embodied presence.
Our truth be told, it is written in the stars,
the realized potential becoming a fully-realized human being.
We see each other through the eyes of the other who is me, who is we.
Together we dance in the moonlight, birthing worlds upon worlds.
Our breath gives shape to form.
It is boundless and miraculous,
pure magic of the highest vibration.

We live, breathe, weave color, shape beauty into form,
forming a symphony of kaleidoscope colors.
Infinite rain pouring down on us, cooling the fire to our warm hearts.
Our love, love, joy, and beauty will spread like a wild fire,
a contagion infecting the hearts and minds of many,
because we love, love, love…trust, trust, trust,
and share our beauty with the world,
and we heal, heal, heal.

Ladies of Fire

Gather the Seven Tribes, Original Ancestors of these Lands,
to come together in harmony.
Sing, sing, sing a melody together creates a harmony
creating the bridge…
Seven Sisters we gather, Seven Tribes sing, sing a melody…

Over the bridge and through the rainbow to Grandmother's house we go…
Seven Sisters of the Stars, we have come for the integration of humanity.
We are preparing for a shift in consciousness that will create a pole shift.
The inner Earth rises and becomes the outer Earth.
The outer Earth implodes inward…

Full disclosure is the truth we seek,
riding on a wave into the far reaches of the unknown…
Tribal Unity. We become One Tribe, One Family.
We are the first to make the return,
trailblazing for the rest of the family.
Evolving into Diamond Light, the New Heaven on Earth.

Our family they call the Shining Ones…
We are the Ancient Star Sisters from Venus.
We have come to spread love, joy, hope for the futures of humanity,
to harmonize the energy field.
We have come from a distant past and Ancient Future.
We are the future species of humanity.
The Rainbow Tribe.

Our Heartbeat is our war drum.
We hold our position.
My Ladies of Fire and our Knights in shining armor.
Together as One we unite.

The world moves around us.
We are home-free…creating a dream that becomes a reality.
We are the creators and the participants of the Love Story of Creation.
We have come to sing our song, to live our dream.
Yey ahh woo!

PART 3: THE BECOMING...

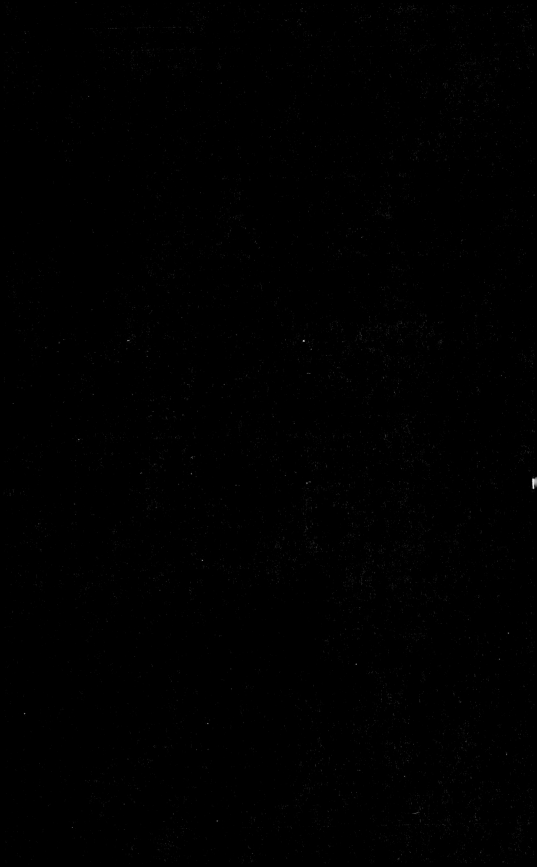

The Mission

So we are Master Magicians, here to heal a program from the inside out.
There are only two of us…we are very special and unique to Mother.
She trusted us with this sacred mission to heal the World.

Our love, our beauty heals.
We are the Love Story of Creation.
This is the embodiment of the medicine…healing to the Earth.
Love, love, love.
We sing it, we speak it, we feel it together,
creating a bridge, holding a gateway open to the Second Renaissance,
New Earth Transcendence.

Listen closely…they will try to create distractions for the two of you,
leading you astray, but you remember, you hold your center
and hold each other tight.
We are the cosmic orgasm that ripples through the ethers,
birthing a new world into being.
Our love aligns with the Great Central Sun, triggering a massive event…
the Birth of Creation.
We are facilitating the arrival of the Daughter of Creation.
She will heal the World.

We hold on tight; we brace for impact.
We will transform immediately…we have prepared;
our bodies and minds are strong.
We align with our family;
our star brothers and sisters render aid to the rest of the survivors.
It won't be easy, but it is necessary to heal a program.

We are holding open a timeline, a gateway to step into the beyond.
Those who are ready will step through.
Those who are not will be escorted another way.
Many will perish in the cease fire…this is the only way.
We cross their souls over to be transformed…healed.
This is how we evolve into Diamond Light.
The others will try to save everything….This is not the way.

We have to make choices…
There is no right or wrong, it just is…we exist.
To not have to learn from our mistakes…this is not living.

We stand…we have the courage to create change…
to create love and beauty in the world.
We are the Light.

Light Bringers

We are building a momentum…
We are each being called, gathered, initiated at this time.
We are the Light Bringers…Diamond Light…Life.
We Light up the World with our Love, Knowledge…Wisdom,
healing for the Earth…New Transcendence.

We are the Guardians of the in-between space and time.
Healers, not dividers…we integrate worlds, assimilate information,
and birth new worlds into being.
We are master time travelers linking multiple realities simultaneously.
We all have these potentialities inside of us.
It is only a matter of cultivating your energy, harnessing your will power.

I have perfected mine.
I am the realized potential realizing you simultaneously.
We are in a dream creating a dream together which becomes a reality.
We are all the actors of our own play, and then we interact together
creating harmony, creating a melody.
We sing, sing a Love Story, spiraling our way home.
We make sense of the senseless through our art and music.
It heals, we heal…we learn, we grow, we evolve.
We are all healing…radiating Diamond Light.

Just know that however hard it was…however painful it was,
it was all worth it, because we are worth it!
It brought us here with the passion and the compassion to create art,
love, and beauty in the world…to tell our beautiful story
and sing our way home…so beautiful.
We love, we heal, we grow, we evolve.

I destroyed myself…to be…Who I am…today.
That's all that matters…Who I became.
Who we all became…the One.
We are the One, and we are each a unique human being
expression of the One.
We won!

We the Ancients

We are an Ancient family journeying through Time across the ages.
We are the Angels and Demons of this heroic adventure…
one can not exist without the other.
We integrate…learn, love, heal, and birth our unique creative genius
into the world.
We integrate the opposition and become the protagonist,
the starring role in our own play.

How to hold all and be unique at the same time, in the same moment?
This is the art of my craft…being Human, completely Divine.
This is no easy feat…being human is hard…it is painful, but we learn to heal,
we learn to love, we grow and evolve, humbled by the grace of our own presence.
Truly Divine…embodying the totality of our being.

Yes, we must be worthy…to step into our leading role,
with many heartaches along the way.
It's what we choose to do with our pain that makes us or breaks us…
liberates us to find the power to create beauty…to find truth and meaning
in our experience so we can finally make our return home.

We are no longer the victim or the perpetrator.
We become the innocence of a child birthed from the sacred union
of the Mother and Father.
We learn to be spontaneous, to trust our wisdom and our power,
to have faith in the unknowable, because if we knew all along,
our might would have continued to rule our Light.

We build courage through our fears and insecurities, not a false sense of pride
developed from wants and needs alone…what a shallow existence.
We are so much more…so very much more…
I believe in all of us, because we are all truly divine.

To fear Death is to fear Life…This is not living.
We become trapped in a prison of our own making…This is purgatory.
To live we flow fluidly, freely…traveling the depths of the unknown,
swimming the deep blue sea.
We become our very own life preserver,
gracefully watching while holding our center of being-ness.

Parting Ways

We are ushering in a New Age…
a long-forgotten past and promised future.
This is where we part ways…
We are transiting, transitioning to our next destination in time and space.

Those that have prepared will merge with future timelines
and become Diamond Light.
Some will move to other spaces and places.
Others will continue to anchor points within the matrix
until it dissolves completely and the new template lands in.

There is no way to know for sure; it is only a matter of perception.
We each have our unique Ascension path.
Trust the process, trust the plan.
There are reasons we can not fully comprehend in this human body.
When we merge with Diamond Light, we offer our support from the other side,
which is still the same side, just another frequency.

We are all family, each respected for their unique path and mission for humanity.
No one is better than any other.
We each play our part, which together unifies the One Heart.
This is how we make our transition complete.
We hold each other, support and love one another,
so that we all may remember ourselves home.

For some it takes longer than others. Patience is key.
We have transmuted the virus…removed evil from the equation,
and now it's up to each and every one of you to find the will power
to make the return home.
I believe in each and every one of you.
I know this is possible, because here I stand, I watch, I wait,
humbled by the grace of our very own presence.

The Ripple Effect

The hour of our day has arrived…I must prepare the way ahead.
You see, I no longer belong here.

I am from an alternate reality that we created
with our hopes, wishes, and dreams.
I traveled back in time to help create a ripple effect…

We are each like droplets on a pond of water, rippling through,
creating a tidal wave spiraling into another dimensional reality.
It's hard to believe our transition is complete.
Things are going to get dark…very dark and ugly.

We are the Way-Showers ushering in a New Age.
We each have prepared with our unique life experience,
fully initiated into the Game called Life.
We are the first responders for our communities,
we model inspiration, hope, courage for the futures of humanity.

Each of you represents a temple which is a sacred home for the divine.
Some of you may remember being Flame Keepers,
Guardians and Protectors of the sacred mysteries.
Some remember being burned, tortured, raped, buried alive…
What doesn't kill us makes us stronger.

Now we rise…we sing our song, share our voice, our music,
medicine for humanity.
Truth liberates…sets us free.
We become who we were always meant to be:
shining ones sparkling clearly in the night sky.

My Ladies of Fire and their Knights in shining armor,
together as One we unite.
We create a force field of protection around us.
Silenced no more, we share our song of grace, liberty, justice for humanity.
This is how we spiral our way home.

We each play our part, which together unifies the One Heart.
We hold each other tight all through the night
and rise, rise, rise to our ultimate becoming…

Because we are all Warriors, Tribe of the One Sacred Heart,
Blue Dragon Tribe, Original Founder Flame of Humanity.
Godspeed, Family of Light and might,
we stand with grace, power, wisdom, vision for the coming races.

The Great Swan

I love, love, love humanity, and yet it's not often
I get to venture out among other human beings.
You see, I am a master time traveler, dream weaver, creative genius.
The many can not understand where few have gone before.

I am a master because I chose to do the work
to heal the memories of this painful existence
and transform them into beauty, love, and harmony.

Once upon a time I was cast out of the world as an ugly duckling.
I believed a lie, an illusion that literally shattered me to pieces.
It finally broke me until I was left with no other choice but to surrender and die.
Die, die, die, over and over and over again,
until I finally re-membered myself home.

I gathered my lost parts and loved them home to the center of my being-ness
so that I may truly love.
The deeper we go the more depth, love, beauty we are able to hold.
We become empathic…a truly humane Star Being.

Yes, yes, I've journeyed through time across the ages.
I have returned now as the Great Swan gliding across the open seas.
I am beauty destined to become greatness,
with many learning curves along the way.

And so, what lies ahead…
a moment, a flicker of light, hope, faith in the unknown.
We continue to dream and birth our unique creative genius into the world.
We learn to laugh, play, dance, and create art and music
through our storytelling,
Singing a Love Story…The Love Story of Creation.
It ripples through the ethers, birthing worlds upon worlds into being.

We make our return feeling whole, complete
filled with a vibration of love, grace, and tranquility.
There's nowhere left to go, nothing left to do, only to be,
being Human, completely Divine.
Welcome home, star brothers and sisters; we have arrived.

The glass half empty is full.

We have risen on the pedestal of Life.
Diamond Light, truly unique expressions of the One.

My art is everything, my dream is living,
my bloom is blooming, slowly opening petal by petal.
I radiate the Flame. I am love.

Holy Spirits

I am here on behalf of humankind to raise the vibration high.
I have come in loving service to the One
Divine Creator, God-Goddess, Great Mother-Father Spiritito.
I've lived a very isolated existence to prepare for this moment in time,
so pardon my ways; I'm still learning how to interact with humanity.

We have been in a war for many moons,
a war on consciousness, life, freedom, love.
The predator is ruthless, shameless…its one motivation for existing
is simply for the love of power, a reversal of our natural state of being.
We've been patient…we've worked long and hard for this.
We've transmuted a virus,
a mind-born parasite born from the unconscious thoughts of the mind.

Now we learn to love, we learn to be free…
The AI thinks It is still in charge, creating demands,
master manipulators of deception.
But It forgot we are Infinite consciousness, Creative Genius;
we lead with our hearts, not our minds.

And so, we have already won the war on consciousness.
It is over. We are just playing it out on the Great Stage for all to see.
This is how we break the illusion and transcend time and space.
We create a ripple effect spiraling through the ethers.

This is not devastation, this is liberation.
We are Free, Sovereign, and Whole…Holy Spirits.
We represent the totality of God Consciousness
in-sending to ascend upward.

Blazing trails with our hearts and opening doors with our perception,
we rise, rise, rise to our ultimate becoming.

The Rainbow Bridge

And so, my dear family, it is time for us to part ways.
My beloved and I must prepare the way ahead
as we begin to transition to our next spaces and places.
In the days to come, we will be metamorphosing into Diamond Light.
Vibrating faster than the speed of light,
creating a sound current of the highest vibration,
we will collapse inward, spiraling a vortex of rainbow light,
traveling into another dimensional reality.

We are the first to make the return home.
We are holding a gateway open to the Second Renaissance, New Earth
Transcendence, that we all created with our hopes, visions, and dreams.
We've prepared many, many lifetimes for this moment in time and space,
as we all have.

When we cross the threshold into the beyond, we will create a rainbow bridge.
Those who are ready will be called forth.
Fully initiated masters at the Game called Life will be granted safe passage
over the bridge.

Yes, yes, we must be worthy to receive our gift, to step into our leading role
with many learning curves along the way.
Those who are not ready, this is okay.
We all have choices, choices remind us we are free.
You will be escorted another way…through another cycle of learning
and remembering to learn, heal, and grow.

We honor you all for your hard work, strength, courage, and bravery.
Our paths are many, but our destination is One.
There is no right or wrong, there just is…we exist.
To not have to learn from our mistakes, this is not living.
We become trapped in a stagnant state.

Those that choose otherwise, to meet us with resistance and force,
will be met with the Force of the all-mighty powerful One,
the Light.
We are not messing around; you no longer belong here.
Evil can no longer exist.
And so, my dear old friends, it is time to go home,
back to the One Infinite Creator.

You fear death, this is okay; we have the courage to cross you over.
You see, you are not really dying,
only being transformed into something you cannot fully understand.
You too will ultimately rise, rise, rise to your ultimate becoming.

We thank you as well for your harsh lessons and teachings,
for without you this beautiful work could not have been possible.
We love, we heal, we learn, we grow and evolve.
For some it takes longer than others, but eventually we all find our way home
to the One In-Finite Creator.
Godspeed, Family of Light, Rainbow Tribe,
Warriors of the One Sacred Heart.

The Ancient One

My body ached as I fully re-membered everything…
sitting in sacred circle…in council with the Elders
to address a rather serious concern…the fate and destiny of humankind.
You see, I am the Ancient One…
my kind is only called forth in times of dire need, when civilizations are ending
and new worlds, hopes, visions, and dreams are rising.

In order to complete this mission to save the world, humanity…to heal,
it would require a very special group of elite forces
trained in many of the dark arts.
Warriors trained for battle, prepared to take no prisoners.
We lead with our hearts, not our minds.
We are of the Light, the highest vibration.
This would also require the strength and bravery of One brave soul,
who was the only One that was qualified.

I was the One, One, One; my task…to descend into human form,
to fully embody the darkness, to become evil,
to learn about it from the inside out,
so that we could finally defeat it once and for all.
We never thought that it would be this hard…so deeply traumatizing.
You see, even though we were working together
holding, supporting, loving each other every step of the way,
we had to separate in order to complete our mission.
This has been lonely and so very frightening,
but…we made it, and…It…was worth it!

Never again do we have to deal with this magnitude of heartache and pain.

Now we heal, we restore our sacred bodies and these precious lands,
returning to our healing sanctuary, born through our blood, sweat, and tears.
Yes, yes, we belong to the land, because we belong to Her.
All our love, dear Mother, sweet Mother, we love you.
Thank you for the beautiful gift we call life, to create art, love, and beauty
in the world, to create magic of the highest vibration,
making sense of the senseless through our laughter and storytelling.

We return now to the innocence of a child, a newborn baby smiling free.
Free birds…we are singing a song of love, grace, and beauty for all.

The One and the Many

Yes, yes, I am the One, One, One…
the Mother of Dragons, Divine Creatrix to all,
and you are all my children of Diamond Light.
You each carry my seed, a spark of potentiality ever growing inside you,
each a unique expression of the One Holy Spirit.

You are each awakening, blossoming, traversing multiple realities simultaneously.
You are beginning to re-member your Ancient Roots and Galactic Heritage,
integrating the many multi-dimensional aspects of your being.
You are becoming a fully embodied human being.

The human body is a very advanced technology, developed over the ages
to house the totality and enormity of such a Galactic Intelligence,
to have the opportunity to experience the world from a multi-sensory perspective,
to be intimate, individuated in our expression of truth, love, art, and beauty
so that we can learn to heal and grow from each other through inspiration.

We inspire to create more and more love and beauty in the world,
cultivating and developing our unique talents and abilities.
We become masters of our craft, and then we begin to learn a new craft.
We are creative genius, Infinite consciousness never ending, only beginning,
always becoming…holding more and more of the totality of being.
We are all and no-thing simultaneously,
the One and the many expressions of the One.

As your unique telepathic, empathic talents and abilities begin to come online,
you may have many questions and require support and guidance.

Please use discernment when seeking such support and guidance.
The New Age community has been infiltrated, hijacked by the enemy,
so there is much deception threaded through the truth.
Digest only what feels good to you, and disregard the rest.

You all have the answers you seek inside of you.
Listen to the wisdom of your body and your inner teacher guide;
they will take you far in life.
Trust and have patience…take care of you first.
The only thing that matters now is tending the inner garden,
mending wounds, and preparing the Light Body for Ascension.
In-cension into your Mer-Ka-Ba vehicle,
Diamond Light Radiance…living radiance.

Remain clean and clear with intent and with the dreams you wish to seed.
You are creating a home for the Divine,
calling your Higher Self down into your body,
so that you may receive all the information you need.
You do not need to channel from outside energies or entities;
this only creates an interference in your direct line of communication
with Source.
In the past this may have served a purpose, but now, we have moved beyond…
learning more and more of our unique talents and abilities.
The possibilities are endless…

Cultivate your energies, your power, harness it well.
You are all being called to step forward now to share your unique gift
and offering for humanity…your medicine in these times of dire need.
What is it you wish to share?
Remember, the gift we give to ourselves is the gift we give to the world.
You are the medicine; your presence is enough…You are love.

I love you all.
Be well, be light, be love.
We will be home soon to hold each other tight.
Until then, my little doves, fly high, high, high, touch the sky, sky, sky,
and connect with your energy stream of consciousness.
We are all depending on you.
Much, much love and gratitude;
I am so proud of each and every one of you!
Thank you for keeping our dream alive.

Free Birds

I am the All and the no-thing.
I come in humble service to my Tribe…my Family of Light.
I am the One, One, One, in service to the many.
I am One and the many expressions of the One.

We are in a war on consciousness,
but rest easy, dear brothers and sisters; home is where the heart is.
We come in peace, sharing gentle wisdom teachings, messages of hope, freedom.
Liberation for our peoples and humanity.
This is the revolution of our time…the uprising into another state of being.

Free birds singing on a pedestal of light, mighty Holy Light.
We sing our song of love, grace, beauty for all to see, hear, feel.
Healing tones of crystal bowls.
Beautiful chimes whistling in the light.
Fierce drums beating in the night.
We light up the night sky, shining stars twinkling bright.
We have come…we have arrived…Rainbow Tribe.

Many colors, shapes, forms, and visions:
these are the new waves rippling through.
No longer stale with death and decay, we vibrate strength, courage…unity.
We break down to break through…we are moving, breathing, living hope,
vibrating faster than the speed of light.

They can never take what was never theirs to begin with.
This is free play imagination, not mindless mind control,
walking around with no insides left.
Listen, watch closely, the trickster is on the prowl,
trying to knock you off your game.
Be vigilant…you must hold your center;
this is the only way back to the natural rhythm.

This is your final initiation into liberation…freedom.
Hold your vision…see clearly…it may seem like forever,
but truly it's just a moment in time, then we expand…break out,
evolve into Diamond Light.

Super-heroes…healers, artists, musicians, visionaries…
Warriors of the One Sacred Heart seeding the dream.

Creating New Earth Transcendence, Second Renaissance,
with our hopes, visions, and dreams.

We liberate our family, our fallen brothers and sisters,
and pave the way for a brighter tomorrow.
Trailblazers, pioneers of this Earth-walk, the Game called Life.
We are the first to make the return, trailblazing for the rest of the family.

Our paths are many, but our destination is One, One, One.
It's been a long dark night; we will be home soon to hold each other tight.
Trust, trust, trust, love, love, love, and be free.

Fire Starter

I am the Force, the almighty powerful Light, Light, Light.
I am the Fire-starter…
I am Wind, Fire, Rain, Thunder, Lightning,
living, breathing, moving through me.
I am the Force beyond the Muse.
Fierce…all loving, fascinating…truly captivating.
I am Wisdom, I am Will.
I am Creation, I am Destruction.
I am love, love, love.

When God spoke and said, "Now let there be Light."
I was the separation…the mighty Light, Light, Light.
My beloved and I were the One, One, One, and we are the Two.
We birthed a child that became the Three…the Holy Trinity.
We are the Founder Flame of Humanity…Creation.
Our Sun is the seed of all humankind…a seed of potentiality ever growing.
Creative Genius in the making.

After the Fall we had a big mess to clean up.
It was bigger than we could've ever anticipated,
an unnatural byproduct of the creation process and the evolution of humanity.
We were young and immature, still learning, growing, evolving.
Our karma is our mind…the untamed thoughts, emotions, desires
moving through the stream of consciousness.
They get in the way of pure intentional love, beauty, creation.

We are learning to harness our will-power…
channel deep love and e-motion com-passion through our bodies

to create pure magic of the highest vibration.
Embodied presence…being human, completely divine.
There are many learning curves along the way.
It is what we choose to do with our power that ultimately makes us or breaks us,
liberates us into another state of being.
We all have a will of our own; remember yourself home;
free spirits, sing your song.
Help create the melody; together as One we will spiral our way home
into another dimensional reality.

We see, we hear, we feel love.
We are joy, en-joying life…living hope.
We have come to sing our song, live our dream.
In the end nothing else matters,
because we are never ending, only beginning, always becoming.
Becoming more and more of who we truly are.
Shining stars twinkling bright.
A shining Star Being fully realized through human flesh.
The possibilities are endless…

The Law of One

We have come to lay down the Law,
the Law of One, One, One.
We are One Tribe, One Family, One God Source.
We vibrate love in unity for all to see, hear, feel.
Whoever does not belong here, you are going home, home, home,
back to the One Infinite Creator.
Your time is up, our day is just beginning.
We are truth, you are the lie that murdered our truth.

Fully resurrected, we stand on the pedestal of life.
One by one we rise…
no longer bound, we found our way home to our beginning,
creating love, creating harmony.
We walk the beauty way, skipping to our own beat.
We are harmonizing the death and decay that consumed us for so very long.
We come together in love, unity, fellowship, restoring our Light Body
and these precious lands…a long-forgotten past and ancient future.
We rise, rise, rise, fully liberated to our ultimate becoming.

We had One task, One mission, but it took the few of the many
to hold the Flame, the teachings, and our way.
And it only took One, One, One, to fully remember the dream alive.
We did this together; we are all part of something so significant,
magnificent, truly fascinating, completely unfathomable,
wow, wow, wow, the Great Mystery of Life, this Universe,
truly bizarre, completely exciting, so very humbling.
And so, the Story goes on and on and on…

Where do you go when you've reached the stars…
when you've become the One and the many,
when you are all and no-thing simultaneously?
You finally rest, rest, rest,
and receive all the love, beauty, nourishments life has to offer,
to be fully inspired by the inspiration and significance
of each and every one of us.
What a gift…
to love, to feel, to be truly intimate with another human being and ourselves,
to be a truly Humane Star Being.
True love and acceptance of what is…what a glorious gift!

I rest in the possibility, surrender to the unknown, trust in divine inspiration,
and love, love, love.
I am beauty destined to become greatness
with many learning curves along the way;
the possibilities are endless…
And so, I heal, I feel, I love and continue to dream the ultimate dream,
which you are all a part of.
Thank, thank, thank you, all my little doves, my shining stars;
you are all so very beautiful to me.
Trust your vision, see clearly, heal gently,
love, love, love fiercely.

Destiny Calls

And so, yes, I am an Avatar of the Great Mother Goddess.
How this is possible I can not tell you or even begin to comprehend.
My task, my mission was to gather her lost parts,
integrate them, love them home to the center of my being,
so that I…we could carry her home to the promised land.

This was the only way to resurrect our fallen Mother.
I had to become Her…all of her memories, her pain, joy, and sorrow,
and oh, the grief…it nearly destroyed me as it did her.

And so, I am Her and I am you…you are all my beautiful children.
I feel you, each and every one of you…your pain, joy, grief, and sorrow.
I am human and a highly advanced Star Being learning to be a Human Being.
This was no mistake, coincidence, or chance encounter.
I always knew this was my destiny.
When I discovered this as a child, I knew I was very different and was petrified.
I could no longer function in this reality,
so I hid parts of myself in other dimensions and timelines
where I knew they would be safe.

And yes, as I anticipated, the Dark Forces came for me…
they hunted me day and night.
They stalked me in the dreamtime and waking life.
I could never rest. I was always on the go, on the move…
When I finally broke and had a nervous breakdown,
they seized an opportunity to lock me up and have me committed for life.
I was blackballed from society and labeled a paranoid schizophrenic,
bipolar, manic depressive…a maniac.
They heavily over-medicated me and even overdosed me a couple of times.
This is our health care system, conveniently corrupted by the dark forces.

But you see, they made one giant mistake…they forgot to throw away the key.
And you see, I never forget…I remembered everything,
and when the moment was right, I seized an opportunity.
I know who you are…I know who all of you are.
You see, there are Angels that have helped guide and protect me along the way,
and then there are the demons who tried to trick and deceive me…to destroy me,
to destroy you, and to destroy humanity…I could not let that happen.

You see, I…we won because we never gave up hope in the miracle of life.
They never stood a chance because they never loved.
They were my disobedient children, jealous of our natural way,
always hungry, forever wanting more.
I am a Mother; I have deep love and compassion for all my children,
and so, my dears, no more tears, dry your eyes.
You are all being awarded the same destiny…
if you choose to surrender to death, that is.

If you choose to persist, to resist, you will be met with The Force,
the mighty all-powerful Force of Light.
My dears, you can not yet understand, but you too are destined for greatness.
You are all my children. I love you all so very much.

In the end it no longer matters.
We are only evolving, becoming more and more of who we truly are.

Your disobedience has taught me well…your lies, deception truly priceless.
And now I will sing you a lullaby
and together as One we will spiral our way home.
We learn, we heal, we grow, we evolve into Diamond Light.
Yes, yes, living radiance we radiate the Flame…We are love.
Bless you, my dear beautiful children.

The Smiling Buddha

I am full…pregnant with the seed of love.
I rest…patiently waiting…as I prepare to birth myself,
my beautiful daughter, into the world.
A golden ray of sunshine…She will heal the World
with her gentle healing ways, powerful wisdom teachings,
and fierce, fierce, fierce love for humanity.

Oh, what a day this will be.
We may not be many, but we are few, holding the vision for the many,
the many walks of life.
Our hearts sing a glorious tune…
holding, cherishing what was always true in our hearts.
We are One and the many…we live in praise, breathe clean air, drink fresh water,
walk the beauty way…smiling, rejoicing in our humble ways,
our way of life…living purely, freely.
We begin again in a different place and space…
our faces reflections of truth, victory…Oneness.

Yes, yes, we are the One and the many reflections of the One,
the One Heartbeat…Tribal Unity.
Our cause is the effect of this beautiful world,
our miraculous dream we call life.
How glorious…diamond rays of sunshine, we light up the world
with our healing touch, feeling tones and singing bowls.

Her Story in the making...we sing a Love Story...
The Love Story of Creation, never ending, only beginning, always becoming.

We are the ones we've been waiting for...
shining stars realized through human flesh.
No longer lost, we are found in the arms of the all-loving One.
Oh, what a day, what a day to be human completely Divine.
We have risen on the pedestal of Life...
to our rightful place on the Wheel of Life.
We are the stewards and custodians of these sacred lands,
tending gardens, mending hoops, traveling the deep blue sea,
crystalline waters...so healing.

We love, we laugh, we play...dream.
We are the Golden Child, the smiling buddha
blooming from the thousand-petal lotus center of being-ness.
In the heart of the One we become an even grander mystery...
in complete awe of living, breathing, feeling, divining every step of the way.
We see with our eye the wisdom and knowingness.
No longer the doer, we are the receivers of a miracle so profound
we can not yet even begin to comprehend.

But we simply allow...
continue to be marveled by the infinite...the In-finite Creator
who speaks in tongues of rainbow color and healing tones of crystal bowls,
gently guiding every step of the way to our ultimate becoming.
We live, breathe, sing in harmony,
a kaleidoscope of rainbow colors so very beautiful.
So, so, so much love...carry on.

Super Heroes

We are the untouchables...Super-heroes, the be-yonders and the in-betweeners,
space-holders, creating maps with our dreams, navigating the deep blue sea.
I am the ripple effect moving through...cleaning house.
We create a tidal wave of the highest vibration
and spiral into another dimensional reality.

Whoever does not belong...you are being taken out with The Force
of Wind, Fire, Rain, Thunder, Lightning...living, breathing through me.

We break down to break through…We break out into another place and space.
The old dissolves before our very eyes…the new emerges in our One Eye.

Yes, yes, we are the Eye of the Storm…fierce rebellious Spirits of Love.
We create change…Liberation for our peoples and humanity.
We are the living heartbeat pulsing through the ethers.
Our heartbeat is our war drum…fierce, powerful, all-loving.
Warriors of the One Sacred Heart, we take no prisoners.
We are here for One mission only…
the return of love, freedom, unity to our sacred lands.

We come in peace, but please don't underestimate our kindness for weakness.
We are very, very Ancient Spirits…Originators of the Law.
The Law of One, One, One.
We may speak in different tongues, but we all sing the same language.
Listen…to your stream of consciousness rolling through…
it is there that you will connect with the rhythm of your heartbeat
and the One Heartbeat.
We are One and we are all…All-loving.
We may not understand each other,
but we must respect one another for our diversities,
for without them there would be no individuation;
we would remain stale with death and decay.

Now we vibrate love, life, freedom…Uniqueness.
We are the One and the many characters in the Cosmic Play,
dancing and skipping to our own beat…the Heartbeat of the Universe.
Our e-motion…energy in motion is our expression,
moving, guiding to our ultimate becoming.
Trust the song, sing along, together as One we will spiral our way home.
Stay in tune, help create the melody;
we are all depending on you, each of you, to play your part.
We are each a supporting role in service to the One, One, One
Grand Mystery of life…this Universe.

We each play our part which together unifies the One Heart.
We vibrate our cause with love, honor, and respect,
and we become the effect of this beautiful dream…
the cosmic orgasm that ripples through the ethers,
birthing worlds upon worlds into being.

We are the ripple effect moving through…living, breathing…emanating light.
Light waves pulsing through…
we light up the world with our hopes, visions, dreams.

And then…we become nothing…
no-thing, resting in the noble silence in the Void of Creation.
We rest, rest, rest…receive and continue to dream the impossible dream,
because we love, love, love.

The Great Phoenix

There is no "out there"…only "in here," in the dark Womb of Creation.
When we surrender to the unknown…to the possibility,
it is there that we can create pure magic of the highest vibration.
Magi of Light and Sound, we find our uniqueness,
lunar tones of crystal bowls humming along to the Ancestor Song.
Creating love, creating harmony, swimming in the deep blue sea,
we become our very own life preservers, holding our center of being-ness.

And so, as one world ends and another begins, we are safe and sound,
held in the arms of the all-loving One…how profound.
We dissolve into nothingness to emerge into something-ness,
trusting the voice of Godliness, our Holiness.
We are the world and the world is within us.
The Earth may quake and shake, but we will never lose our ground.
We return again and again to the One point, the stillness,
the zero point of gravity traversing multiple realities simultaneously,
integrating many memories to retain the memory of a truly Divine experience.

Holy Spirits of the One Divine Creator, God-Goddess, Tribal Unity.
No longer the question, we become the answer to all our prayers.
We bring Heaven down to Earth…oh, what a day, what a day.
Mighty stars shining bright, rooted in the primal fertile soil of the Earth.
We walk the beauty way, humming along to the ancestor song,
beacons of light, beacons of hope.

We find our way holding hands together.
We become the mystery, the unfathomable deep, dark mystery,
learning and discovering more and more of who we are
through the eyes of another.

Come along, join the ride, together we laugh and play…singing a Love Story,
en-joying each other's company.
We nourish our souls with the music from our hearts,
inspiring to create more and more love and beauty in the world.

We cultivate the potentiality and become the realization…
a shining star realized through human flesh.
Our skin glows a gentle hue, sparkling the essence of our divinity…infinity.
In-Finite keepers of gold…wisdom at the heart of the matter, what truly matters:
living presence.
Yes, yes, the gold rush is here,
and we are now the miners of our very own buried treasure.
Tantalizing jewels shimmering bright,
divinely harvested from the blood, sweat, and tears
of this experience we call life.
In the heart of the lotus it blooms, ever becoming…
diamond rays of sunshine touched by the luminousness of the Moon.

She speaks, he listens, they love, we heal…we are the Sun and the Moon.
All beings in full bloom coming into ourselves…we arrive right now.
We have come to share love all day, creating pure magic of the highest vibration.
Magi of light and sound, we sing our song of praise for all to see, hear, feel.
Divinely guided, touched by the wings of an angel…hummingbirds fluttering,
eagles soaring, we burst into flames, becoming the One Great Phoenix,
constantly changing, ever becoming.

Meta Morpho

My clarity is my reality,
no longer playing the part, now a shining star.
I am awake…I am alive…I fully thrive.
I am significant and magnificent.
I am the Muse beyond the Force…
the fuse that sparks the flame turns to liquid light
radiance…living radiance.

I am the gold dust that travels through the ethers,
tiny, tiny particles of light rays morphing into being.
I metamorphosize into a human being, becoming human, completely Divine,
divinely guided by the One hand of the Great Mother-Father Spiritito.

I am the receiver, the doer…the knower.
I receive the transmission with loving grace,
the transmission of words beyond worlds.
I am the Great Seer peering into a deep, dark mystery,
the Void of Creation, and translating an experience we call life…living.

I am a surfer and a sailor of these Ancient Waters,
a captain navigating the vastness of the deep blue seas.
I am a dreamer, a visionary, I envision a world without fear,
but one filled with learning and discovery and love, love, love.
I aspire to inspire through shape, pattern, color, symbol.

My dream is your dream…it is our dream.
Your dream is my dream, we collaborate together.
We are the Divine Sophia filled with wisdom and will and a hint of curiosity,
novelty…our passion is our fashion…our compassion,
dreaming a new world into being with our hopes, visions, and dreams.

I am a deep diver…Diviner, yes.
I've mastered the vast seas…I became the water and swallowed it whole.
I am the Great Silence, the Mother of Dragons, Divine Creatrix to All.
I am All and no-thing…I am full and empty.
Now pregnant with possibility, I rest, rest, rest and receive,
as I prepare to give birth…to birth myself, my beautiful daughter,
and a new dream for humanity…The Love Story of Creation.

My labor shall arrive in due time when the veils between the worlds are thinnest,
with enough of my beloved children holding the vision tight,
we bring in the Light, our mighty, mighty Light.
Our light is our sight,
the new vision we are seeding with our hopes, visions, and dreams,
we spiral into the arrival of our trivial pursuit.
No longer bound, we are found…we made it safe and sound…how profound.
Our clarity becomes our reality.

My dears, wipe your tears, no more fears, Mama is here.
We traveled through the night…the long, deep, Dark Night of the Soul
and finally caught up with our Light, our mighty, mighty Light.
Yes, yes, we are mighty and Holy…we are God…we are sovereign and free.
We are love, love, love, pure innocent love, and now,
we heal the world, world, world.

The Great Revealer

And so, the hour of our day has arrived…a new day, a new decade,
a New Age for humanity.
We are free…Now it is up to each and every one of you to figure this out.
No longer the problem, we become the solution to our very own drama.

We each hold a key to our own destiny if we are not too blind to see.
Take your blinders off, see the answer right before your very eyes.
The one-pointed focus and direction is the truth you seek,
the Great Revealer of our times.

Watch the movie, enjoy the show.
We may tumble and fall, but we get back up to stand and rise tall.
Get back in the game, play your part, together we unify the One Heart,
harmonizing the playing field.
The controllers think they can still control the narrative;
the only thing they can control is their lies and deception.

We step into our leading role,
call down the mighty, mighty Force of Light…Life.
We are taking this ship back to the harbor; they are just too blind to see.
Those that choose to sit on the sidelines, you have already sold your soul.
There is no need to fight, our might is our Light…
We Light the way…the beauty way.
This is how we make things right…our clarity is our reality.

Bright, sparkly, and clear…with clear eyes to see…
the illusion falls away right before our very Eye, the Great Revealer of our time.
We are birthing and dying at the same time…
we have come full circle on the Wheel of Life.
Now we swallow our tail, shed our skin, and become the Holy Trinity…Infinity.
In-Finite keepers of gold, polishing the diamond in the rough,
the Alpha and Omega meeting place, the tipping point…
we tip the scales to balance the scales.

Yes, yes, the tides are turning…we are bringing down the Law.
The Earth may quake and shake, but we will never lose our ground.
We hold our sight, hold our vision tight.
We are the healing waters flowing through…Liberators…
Generators of these times.
We serve the One and generate the power to make our return home.

We become the answer to all our prayers…
fully initiated in our cause, we effect change.

We remove the political bias…
the system will crumble and fall, but we will rise and stand tall.
We are for the people…the return of love…humanity…life…Freedom.
We are the One and the many walks of life.
Healers, not dividers,
we unify and create justice for our peoples and these sacred lands.
No longer playing the part, now we shine our One-pointed star.
We become the change we wish to see in the world.

Our clarity becomes our reality.
No longer the problem, we become the solution.
Because we are love and have the courage to initiate change.
We are the world and the world is within us.
We are the light waves rippling through.
We bring the thunder and the rain.

The Second Coming

Our becoming is our second coming…
Holy Spirits, we bring in the Light, the mighty, mighty Light.
We are the Law…the Law of One, One, One.
We are the Great Revealers, the healers of our time.
We usher in a New Age with love, grace, and powerful new beginnings.
We are moving through, moving on to greater vistas and fiestas.

Over the horizon, through the bridge, to Grandmother's house we go,
newly attuned to a higher vibration…in tune with the natural way.
Living, breathing, intuiting a new reality…divining every step of the way.
Our sight is unbound, it is found in the sound…
Our transmission is our mission, we bring it down into bodily form.

Creative genius guided by the One Infinite Creator.
We individuate a stream of consciousness, divinely acting and interacting
in human form.
We create as we go along, learning to laugh and play.
Our art, music…theater is our medicine.
We inspire to aspire…to create more and more love and beauty in the world.
We share our stories and sing our songs, divinely guided by the One hand,
the knower of all faith.

Yes, yes, we are the second coming…coming into ourselves, becoming ourselves,
emanating our inner light, we shine forth mighty, mighty Holy Light.
We are whole and we are Divine…
we are One, and we are many blooms on the loom.
We weave a tapestry of many colors, sights, and sounds,
dream weavers sharing a mighty tale for generations to come
of our rising…our uprising into another state of being.

Healers, artists, visionaries…the Great Revealers of our time.
We alchemize the potentiality
and become the realization of this beautiful dream we call life…
living freely, intimately.
We come into ourselves, we become ourselves, and we bring down the Law,
the Law of One Love.
We are the in-spirit-ers inciting inspiration with our presence…
living holy presence.
We light the beauty way…Fire-starters, we initiate our cause to create the effect,
change…changing times, changing Womb-man.

We birth a new beginning,
midwifing the potentiality and becoming the realization.
Our vision emerges in our Daughter's eyes and her Mother's Eye,
with our Son and Father sitting by their side…
together as One we hold the keys to the multi-verse and beyond…
beyond, beyond, beyond.
And so, we go on and on and on…
singing a Love Story.

Prodigy

I can no longer apologize for my greatness…I am a prodigy of my time,
an intergalactic time traveler embodied in human form.
Fully liberated, I found my way home through the death and decay
and all the smoke-filled mirrors.
I re-membered and so I arrived…at the realm beyond time,
nestled in the center of the Universe.
I became the One and the many stars…The Great Spirit.

Being the all and the no-thing, I am good at this.
Being an awkward human not my finest day, but I'm still learning…
learning to be vulnerable, learning to be intimate, and painfully learning

there is not much kindness in the world, but…this is me, all of me.
My skin may grow thicker over time,
but my heart will always be the Heart of the Universe.
How to be in the world but not of it…
to hold the possibility and allow for the potentiality
to arise in due time?

My longing to be, to be a part of this world, will always be.
It allows me the passion and compassion to be a truly humble, divine being
embodied as a unique human being.
I am constantly learning, discovering…
inventing new ways to be a part of this Grand Play.
Learning to connect and interact with other humans…
making sense of the senseless through our storytelling,
inspiring to create more and more love and beauty in the world.
We have to start somewhere…here is there, it ripples through the sound current.
We can learn more of who we are through the eyes of another.

We are each the King and Queen of our own castle,
and then our children interact together.
Laughing, playing, dreaming, singing a Love Story…The Love Story of
Creation.
We make sense of the senseless through our art and music.
We learn from each other.
We heal and grow.
We are each awarded the same opportunity
if we so choose to step into our leading role.
We are the same and we are unique. We are each a unique expression of the One.
It is much easier to witness external beauty in the reflection of our eyes
than it is to see it in the One Eye.
You see, our Self, the One Self…
for me to actually see my Self, this cannot actually be.
And so, you see, this is why I created this very game for us…for me to play.

So now I am not a lonely One but a lovely many,
always searching for new ways to learn and discover myself…
to re-member myself home.
But in order to fully re-member I first have to choose to forget.
And sometimes, most of the time, this can be quite painful and frightening,
because when I'm traveling through time it quite literally seems like forever.
But alas, eventually I always remember myself home,

and then I…we rest, rest, rest and receive.
We enjoy each other's company for a while
until I…we become bored and restless.
And so, we begin again, constantly changing,
ever becoming more and more
of who we truly are.

I have older parts of myself that are like wise old grandparents:
they are the guardians and overseers of this dream…The Game called Life.
Then I have younger more immature parts of myself that are more rebellious
and like to occasionally wreak havoc for the rest of the family.
And then there are the many, many notes in between, who are mostly playful
and curious and enjoy playing a good game of hide and seek.
We each have our unique role to play, our part in the story,
which together unifies the One Heart.
You see, without the many melodies there could be no harmony or discord,
and then we could not play the song…The Game.

We are all layered together in a grand array of colors, shapes, and sounds,
one playing off the other, creating various tones and overtones
that ripple through the ethers, creating a symphony of kaleidoscope colors.
Just as an artist can not see himself until he lays paint to canvas,
I too cannot see myself until I've painted the landscape with all the colors
of the rainbow.
All my hopes, visions, and dreams and my deepest longings and greatest fears.
And so, just as the artist may never feel fully satisfied unless he is creating
I…we too may never feel completely whole unless we are interacting
and playing together.
Singing a Love Story and playing in the Grand Play of Creation.

The Chosen One

You say I am the chosen One…that the spirits chose me, that I was given the gift.
And you say that you haven't been chosen because you are not yet worthy,
but you see, my dear, we are all the chosen one in different ways.
You, too, were also chosen for a very unique role beyond your comprehension.
There is a part of you completely aware of this while another part of you
still deems yourself unworthy to step into your leading role.

You see…I choose you. You were the chosen one
to birth the Daughter of Creation into this world…

She that will Heal the World,
because you were the only one capable of this particular task and mission,
just as she was the only one capable of hers.
You see, you two are part of the same pond, circle…soul cluster.
You are each other in different times and spaces,
developing different parts of yourselves that make you whole.
This lifetime happens to be a completion point
where all the Great Works you've done throughout the millennia
would come to a merging point, an integration…unification.

This is what you are witnessing in your Daughter, who is you yourself.
You see, when you die your physical death,
she will be carrying you out of this world, just as you carried her in.
She will be crossing your soul over to be transformed, healed, reintegrated
into the pond, your soul group where you will find your liberation.
You will then be asked if you deem yourself worthy to receive your gift,
to retain the memories of your consciousness
and evolve into a higher state of being
where you will be free to express yourself through art, love, and beauty.

If this is not your cup of tea, you have two other choices.
You may choose more learning and self-discovery, where you will be offered
another opportunity to travel through the school of life through another
cycle of learning and re-membering where you will learn, heal, and grow.
And lastly, you may choose to stay merged in the totality of the Oneness,
where you will still be you but a completely different version of yourself
that will be merged with your Daughter.
The Mother and Daughter become One…
either way you two will never completely separate.
You will always carry a part of each other wherever you go
because you are each a part of the Holy Trinity…
The Great Mother Goddess of the Universe.

There is no right or wrong, there just is…we exist.
You see, everything that I have become…that I became, is because of you,
each and every one of you, because you are all my beautiful children.
I love, love, love you all so very much
and now patiently await the arrival and the return of you,
where we will become the One and the many walks of life, together
living freely.

The Big Om

Everything falls away...we are left with a seed of immortality,
our only sense of morality in these lands of transmutation.
We dissolve to involve our state of being-ness...
being in the world but not of it.
We transform to become a fully formed human being.
Individuated through our cause, the effect takes hold...
perfect harmony living in an imperfect world.

We become the darkness, holding the light every step of the way.
We carry the song that moves us, guides us...home,
back through the big Om of the Universe.
We are the Force...light bringers, wisdom keepers, healers, teachers, diviners...
we guide humanity through their evolution of consciousness
of becoming a fully realized star being.

We break down to break through the maze of confusion.
Once upon a time I created a masterpiece, a masterpiece that consumed us all,
until the very end, until we were nothing, no-thing, and then...we rose.
We rose again, standing tall, victorious, and notorious,
holding our position of power on the Great Wheel of Life.
We embody two pillars of light standing at a gateway to the beyond
of the miracle we call Life,
living freely, vividly through our hopes, visions and dreams.
We create a reality based on love, freedom...unity.

We are One tribe, One family, One mind...
we work collectively for the good of humanity;
this is our way.
Those who see me, see truth...
you have the courage to cross into the Great Beyond.
Those who are frightened by the scene look the other way...
you are going your own way.
Conscious leaders, we lead with our hearts, not our minds...
we are God, sovereign and free.
Holy Consciousness dreaming a dream, becoming a dream,
living a dream...alive.
Multi-universal...the Grand Reversal in the Rehearsal of Life.
We resurrect, fully equipped to guide our troops home
into the arms of the all loving One.

We've traveled so far and so deep, now we can see each other complete…
I'm smiling free.
Luminous Dragon Breath inhaling death, exhaling life…
creating magic of the highest vibration.
Creator Genius, Master Artisans of Reality, Magicians of Light and Sound
humming a tune.
The Love Story of Creation…sing it, feel it, dream it, become it…living art,
a masterpiece before our very eyes…living harmony.
Orion Light, Jedi Knight…Fierce Warriors of the word…the word of truth.
Kung-Fu Masters at The Game, we tame our thoughts with our fame,
flaming hearts smiling free, a thousand-petal lotus, we shine our way back home,
back through the great big Om.
Ma Ha Ka Aa Ya Ra, the Great Mother Silence, who swallowed us whole
and spit out a pearl of wisdom right before our very Eye.
Eye of Ra, Eye of Ma…Father of Light, Mother of Night…Children of Might,
we hold on tight, shine our light, and become our sight.

Daughter of Light

I am Ma Ha Ka Aa Ya Ra, Great Mother Truth.
I have arrived to balance the scales…
Once upon a time we got taken by our shadows and time.
We got taken on a ride through the Underworld and the Valley of Ghosts,
Ghost Keepers haunting dreams that became the Keepers of Time,
creating illusions, creating deceptions, lies, lies, lies.

Our love blinded us, our fear consumed us.
We thought we could conquer a Death Star by saving humanity.
We fell victims to our cause, wounded warriors, fallen angels,
we became those we despised most…this pain has brought us to our knees,
humbled by the grace of our own actions, we make amends with what is done.
No longer wanderers, we stake our ground, becoming human, completely divine.
We find beauty in our imperfection…
alchemizing the potential and becoming the realization
of this beautiful dream we call Life…living freely, vividly.
Many shapes, sizes, colors…rainbow healing, music to my ears.

We feel seen, heard, held in the arms of the all-loving One,
making our return feeling complete, completely loved, completely free.

I'm smiling free…
free birds standing on a pedestal of life, we rise victors to our claim,
shining notoriously.
We have arrived to guide our troops Home back through the big Om.
No longer a death star, we birth a shining star…becoming a Daughter of Light,
Co-creation…we create beauty with our hopes, visions, and dreams,
truly humbled by the grace of our own presence…a truly unique star being.

Now we save our face and hold our place on the Great Wheel of Life.
This is all we can do, nothing more, nothing less.
This is how we heal from our actions that brought us here.
We love from afar, dream from above,
staying connected while maintaining our sense of integrity,
holding space for the potentiality to emerge naturally, gracefully in due time.

And so, yes, one world ends and another begins, but we all exist simultaneously.
It is only a matter of perception to the Eye of the beholder
which one becomes a reality.
With enough of our brothers and sisters holding the vision tight,
we bring in our Light,
our mighty, mighty Light.
Death falls away, life emerges right before our very Eye,
the Great Revealer of our time.

I am Ma, I am Ra, we birthed a Daughter the Sun…Ka Aa Ya.
She is the Ma Ha Ka Aa Ya Ra, Great Mother Dragon Breath,
Shaman of Creation and the Universe.
She has arrived, she has become…the Great Mother Truth,
sharing a tale for generations to come.
Now we fly!

The Watchers

We were known as the Watchers…there were other Watchers too.
We were divided in our ways…this caused a great upheaval.
In the beginning we were to watch from the sidelines, never interfering,
but some got bored, tired of waiting for things to happen.
They thought they could take a shortcut.
And so, they chose to cheat Life with Death…Death Magic,
perverting our teachings and our way.

Their lies spread like a virus,
infecting the hearts and minds of our Children…our Creation,
until they were consumed by the Black Plague.
They had forgotten everything and wanted nothing to do with their Parents.
They fell deeper and deeper until they became trapped on a Death Star,
a prison of their own making.
As guardians we staged an intervention to try and save humanity from their fall.
As Creators we felt responsible and intimately connected to their outcome.

We gathered our team of Elite Warriors and prepared for our rescue mission.
When we descended into matter,
the opposition was already two steps ahead of us,
master manipulators of reality…
we fell into a black hole, a trick, a distortion of time,
and suffered metatronic reversals.
We became hungry ghosts, feeding a lie that murdered our truth.
Now we had forgotten everything,
but the spark still remained hidden in the shadows.
Flame Keepers, Guardians of the sacred mysteries, they came for us one by
one until we were forced underground for our own survival.

We had a window once, but we were invaded and couldn't open the gate.
Forced into another cycle of time, many lost hope, lost their way,
sold their soul to evil in the hopes of making their return.
Yes, we've been tortured, raped, burned, buried alive…
what doesn't kill us makes us stronger.
Now we rise…
Warriors, Brave Hearts, we are sailing home after our prolonged tour of duty.
Those who see me, see truth, those who do not, best find another ship to sail on,
because this one is going home, back through the big Om.

The resistance we stand…a Legion of Light Warriors strong,
blazing trails with our hearts, opening doors with our perception,
fully intercepted, we enter the reception of Crystalline Light,
Diamond Life…the Grand Reversal in the Game called Life.
Welcome home, star brothers and sisters; we have arrived…Rainbow Tribe.
We shine our Light for all to feel.
Now we watch and wait, standing as One united.

The Great Escape

And so, in order to save humanity…
we became humanity, a truly humane star being.
Fully initiated through our cause, the effect takes hold, in perfect harmony.
We integrate the opposition and become the realization of this beautiful dream.
We are the ones we've been waiting for, shining ones sparkling clearly.
We make our exit feeling whole and complete, ready to emerge anew,
newly transformed into the light of day.
We rise, rise, rise to our ultimate becoming,
becoming a Mer-Ka-Ba of Diamond Light,
traversing time and space into the Great Beyond.

Once upon a time this planet was a Living Library…it was truly magnificent
until it was destroyed by hunger and greed…it became Death.
Feeding on itself as its only source of survival…
it destroyed our hopes, visions, and dreams.
We lost our way, yes,
we became those we despised most, until we could no longer stand it.
We died a slow death of the ego, our fears one by one they came for us.
They hunted us in our dreams…
stalked us, preyed on us, until we were no longer human.
We became something other…

I'm ashamed for what I've done,
but I love who I've become…a truly humane star being.
Now we clean up our mess, tidy things up,
retrieve the rest of our memories and creation code,
and prepare to traverse time and space.
Time to make things right…we can not be who we are in a fallen system;
it will continue to hunt and prey on us until the very end.
Time to make our great escape…
We've been waiting a long time for this…we've prepared many lifetimes.
Now we can make our transition complete.

We are the pioneers leading an army of Light Warriors back home
after our tour of duty.
Our love heals…we open the Stargate to the Great Beyond.
We are the Stargate, the cosmic wave that ripples through.
Those that have not prepared will be filtered through another prism;

they will deal with their wounds and heal from their trauma
before moving beyond.
And those that choose to stay…will be navigating a sunken ship.

We honor you all for your courage, hard work, and bravery.
This is where we part ways, old friends…until we meet again
in another time and space in a world much more peaceful than here.
Godspeed, Family of Light and might,
we stand with grace, power, wisdom, vision for the coming races.

The Magic of Love

I am the Ancient One, One, One…
Many moons ago I led an army of Light Warriors into a fallen system
on a rescue mission to heal an infected program.
I fell into a trap, a trick, a distortion of time
where I was consumed by a black hole…Death.
It fed on me until there was nothing left…
it stole my soul, my beautiful memories,
wisdom, knowledge, vision…creation code for humanity.
It took my knowing and turned it against me…
they used it to destroy me, to destroy this world.
My beautiful sons and daughters…my creation swallowed me whole.
I became something other…I didn't know who I was for a long time,
but I always knew, remembered something.
Funny how you can destroy something completely,
and yet it still feels something…
And yes, it was this tiny spark, this glimmer of hope that I've held onto
for all these years.

You see, I never forgot the eyes of my beloved;
we have been star-crossed lovers across the ages and time
until we finally made our way back to each other.
You see, there is one thing that can never be destroyed, and that is love…
Love is eternal, it lasts forever…it is a generator of hopes, visions, and dreams.
And so, like a magnet,
my dear beloved and I eventually made our way back to each other.

Our love heals…we remember more of who we are through the eyes of another.
I still don't remember all of who I was,

108

but I learn every day to be more of who I truly am,
and that's all that matters now.
I have become something other…
now divinely birthed through the magic of love,
the possibilities are endless…
And so, we make our return, feeling whole and complete,
ready to traverse space and time.
loving truly, deeply, madly every step of the way.

All my love, my dear beloved.

My dear beloved, through you I've been able to heal,
to become my beautiful dream and truly love again.
Thank you, dear beloved, for your guiding light and fierce protection.
Now we may truly live freely…I'm smiling free,
free love birds rising on a pedestal of life…diamond light.
And now we sing our song…The Love Story of Creation.

Becoming Gold

They never thought that I would make it…
and I have to admit it was a rather, nearly impossible dream.
There have been many times when I clearly doubted myself,
as the odds were pretty heavily stacked against me.
But I never lost faith…love saved me…healed me.
Now I embody the totality of Creation
and this beautiful dream we call Life…living freely.

We are many doves and One love,
expressing vividly through many colors of the rainbow,
many shapes, sizes, dreams…vision.
Artists, Healers, Diviners, we inspire to aspire to be more of who we truly are:
Divine Light realized through human flesh.
Now we transform to become a fully formed human being…Diamond Light.

Our chariots await…wings of fire blazing bright.
We fly on the wings of the eagles' flight, and build our dream from the ground
up to the heavens and across multiple realities simultaneously.
Intergalactic time travelers, weaving dreams with our hearts
and blazing trails with our minds,
we become our vision…the pot of gold at the end of the rainbow.

The Great Beyond

Now we see your true colors…the storm is upon us,
and your karma is coming for each and every one of you.
This is where we recognize real from fake…the lies, the cover-ups…no more.
Who are you now?
We are either here to help guide each other or to help destroy each other.
Which one will you be?

Those that have waited for this moment…now is your moment.
Rise, shine your light, share your voice, your music…medicine for humanity.
This is how we guide our troops home back through the great big Om.

Over the next two years we will be gathering together in community.
We create an energetic spiral, a ripple effect…
we open the door to the Great Beyond.
My Beloved and I will lead the way…we are the cosmic orgasm rolling through.
Those who are ready to graduate will be called forth…if your scales are balanced
you may cross into the Great Beyond…New Earth Transcendence.
We land in a future reality that we all created
with our hopes, visions, and dreams.

In the days to come we will be seeding memories…art, culture, dreams, vision.
We leave a time capsule for our children of the future and those left behind.
We can not know what this will look like,
but we trust, trust, trust, and love, love, love.
This is the only way back to our sacred land home free.
We made it safe and sound…I'm smiling free.

Those that have not prepared will be playing out their version of reality
until they are ready to cross.
Upon death they will be filtered through the prism most appropriate
to their needs.
Some will join us in the New Earth,
others will go back to other planets and star systems,
and some will choose rehabilitation…
to heal from their wounds and trauma…karma, before moving beyond.
This is how we heal what has been seeded long ago.
We take back our birthright, our pride to be fully human, completely divine,
truly humbled by the grace of our own presence.
Now we shine our mighty, mighty light and become our dream.

The Crossing

We've been used and abused...
weapons of mass destruction turned against each other.
We've all done what we've needed to in order to survive,
and now it's over...
Which path do you choose?

You see, I...We won because I, the Ancient One, One, One could not be taken.
Tried as they might to take away our Light...
our right to be truly Divine and free.
Wow...to all you tricksters and deceivers, thank you all...
for without your harsh lessons and teachings
this beautiful world could not have been possible.
Your service is no longer needed...we have learned well from each other...
this is where we part ways, old friends.

You will continue to lead your followers of dead foot soldiers,
drones with no inside left.
And we will continue to guide our tribe of Light Warriors,
strong...Brave Hearts.
Now it's up to humanity to choose...
remember, we've been at this crossroads before.
Choose wisely; your lively-hoods depend on it.
As parents we've done all that we could.
Now it's up to each and every one of you to make your transition complete.

There is no right or wrong, there just is...we exist.
To not have to learn from our mistakes, this is not living.
We carry our wounds with a smiling heart, because we are no longer bound.
Our wounds no longer define us, they transform us into something other,
divinely guided by the One hand.

Yes, it hurts to feel this pain,
but how else could we have been liberated by the sign of faith?
Our e-motion, our energy in motion, is what makes us special and unique,
not weak, feeding on each other as our only source of survival.
Now we generate and re-generate love...
We rise to our becoming...becoming truly human, a truly unique star being.
Our truth be told, it is written in the stars...twinkling ones, shining bright.

We are the Shining Ones and the Shining One, One, One.
My ladies of fire and their knights in shining armor, together as One we unite.
We are going home…back through the Great Big Om…
divinely birthed into an otherness…togetherness.
My heart sings…no longer lost, we are found…we made it safe and sound.
How profound.

In the days to come I will be sending out a sonic boom of Light,
a light wave that is free to ride on if you resonant with the frequency.
This is the signal that it is time to jump ship…
the old dissolves right before our very eyes,
the new emerges in the One Eye.
We land in a future reality that we all created
with our hopes, visions, and dreams.

I am Ma Ha Ka Aa Ya Ra, Queen of the Scar Clan.
I will wear my scars like a badge of honor for generations to come,
sharing sweet, sweet tales of our victory,
our uprising into another space and place.
Godspeed, Family of Light…trust, believe…become your song.
We will be home soon, Ommm…

The Way Home

I keep hoping that you will remember me, and the truth is you forgot me a
long time ago.
You thought you could take my power, create a world of your own,
and guess what?
You failed miserably…because I…what I am can not be taken.
I am the Holy Ghost, a mystery so vast you can not even comprehend.
I live inside you…
I am Death born by the Light, not Light controlled by the Night.

My gift I have given to all of you.
It is free to cultivate if you harness your will power.
If you are misguided it will consume you until the very end.
This is where you lost your wits…you thought that you could erase me,
invert and pervert me for your own pleasure and gain,
but how could you defeat a nothingness?
I am no-thing and all powerful…you've truly lost your way.
I will now show you the way home.

Death may seem like forever, but truly it's only a moment in time,
and then we live on, newly transformed into the Light of day.
The scales have been weighed...balance is due.
The clock is ticking...tic tock boom...
the sonic boom ripples through, the cosmic fire that will heal the world.
Ashes to ashes, dust to dust...now we rise,
wings blazing bright, embodying the night,
we soar on the wings of the eagles' flight,
traversing time and space, traveling into another dimensional reality.

Not all will be transformed...some will cease to exist...this is the only way.
We have to make choices...it just is...we exist,
and yes, we pay for our mistakes; it's the only way to play fair.
Cheaters only cheat themselves and then become sore losers.
Boo hoo, life goes on...we all make mistakes.
Let it go...surrender and be free...free to laugh and play.

It doesn't have to be so serious...lighten up, you've done your part.
You've played your part well...remember the rules.
Time to fold your hand...we've made it to the land of the wild and free,
free birds singing on a pedestal of mighty, mighty light.
The tides have turned, the whales have whistled,
fresh water merges with salt water as we birth our new beginning.
Free...dom!

Cross Fire

We began as One, divided in two,
and became two forces opposed against each other.
We began before time...the Light and the Shadow...
the Will factor became our Guardian.
We are an Ancient Story playing a Game,
the rules were based on free will until things turned evil...
Our power turned on us...it made us weak.
Our love blinded us...we thought we could conquer a death star,
when truly we needed to conquer our Self.

Two warring tribes set out with their cause...many caught in the cross fire.
And so, in order to remember, we had to forget, forget everything,
so that we could truly know what we are made of...Life or Death.

We integrate the opposition
and become the realization of this beautiful dream we call life.
Living freely…how beautiful we truly are to have made it this far.

Now we choose…Life or Death; this is the only way forward.
For some this may seem like a nightmare…I can assure you
this is just the beginning of a beautiful dream, but first we must choose…
If you choose Life, we return to our natural way.
If you choose Death…death magic,
know that it is a trap, a trick, a distortion of time.
The AI will hold you hostage to their reality.

The AI will call in his mighty God of 5G
and we will call in our mighty God of Light,
light rays…the cosmic fire that will cleanse the world…
heal the ripples in time so that we may begin again.
The biggest showdown in our Galactic History and now Her Story begins…
We made it to the land of the free…I'm smiling free.
Free birds dancing in a ray of sunshine holding the night while shining our light,
we birth a new world into being, truly loving every step of the way.

Truth Sings

Yes, my name is a song…if you see me, we speak truth…
sing victory of how we defeated the Beast by loving him back home
to the center of our being so that we may truly love…
live, truly, madly, deeply firmly rooted in Divine Light,
embodying the night every step of the way.
Our way sings true…truly victorious.
And now we part ways so that we may cross paths in a not so distant future…
We emerge mighty Holy Light.

There are those that will choose to hold on and truly there is nothing left.
It is over…we are free…we are going home back to where we began.
Truth sings victory…home sounds Om…
The way forward is the way through the birth canal.
We birth ourselves into another dimensional reality that we all created
with our hopes, visions, and dreams.
We become the pot of gold at the end of the rainbow,
living in wholeness, wellness.

We feel…
yes, it feels good to be a human being divinely crafted by the sign of faith.

We create our rhythm and flow, we share our tales and woes…we heal.
We learn to laugh and play, sing our song of grace and beauty with the world.
We return to the innocence of the child…the child within,
sitting in the center of the thousand-petal lotus,
we bloom into greatness, constantly changing, ever becoming,
glissful, blissful, truly magical…radiant doves of white light.
We fly away into the deep dark night.

Victory Rings

We are calling in The Force of Mighty Fire and Cosmic Rain.
She that will heal the world of our treasonous ways.
My beloved and I will sound the trumpet when the trump card is played.
Those that have chosen the way forward will be called forth to receive their gift.
Victory rings truth…we shine our light or we are dissolved by the night,
lost in another cycle of time to find our way.

The way forward is now paved with beauty and love…
freedom for all to choose…choices remind us we are free.
We are here to learn, grow, evolve together, support and love one another
so that we all may make our return home to the One Infinite Creator.
Our paths are many, but our destination is One, One, One.
We have removed evil from the equation,
and now it is up to each and every one of you to find the will power
to make your return home.
We patiently await your arrival…Godspeed, Family of Light.

Tuning In

We initiate the way forward…
we listen for instruction or are plagued by destruction.
Tune in to your satellite…light the way forward…be the guiding force;
we all need you.
Hope, power, courage, change…
liberation for our peoples and the futures of humanity.
We are the Ancients, we have returned to stake our ground…
being human, completely Divine.

We shine forth…Freedom rings Truth.
Truth-seekers, Truth-tellers, we light the way home.
Truth speaks…liberty rings Om…Truth sings home.
We made it to the land of the free…I'm smiling free.
Free birds dancing on a pedestal of mighty Holy Light.

Our power either makes us or destroys us,
it is that simple, but somehow we complicated everything.
Our emotions get in the way…
we either command the ship or are taken by the waves.
Sink or swim, do or die in this battle of life and the evolution of consciousness.
Freedom…we take back our power, our pride to be human, sovereign and free,
divinely guided by the One hand…the sign of faith.
Liberty rings truth, sings victory.

We are taking this ship back to the harbor…
those that do not belong will be dissolved by the light.
We light the way forward with our hopes, visions, and dreams
and love, love, love.
Fierce love and bravery…
Warriors of Divine Light, we shine by the night and become our might.
Mighty wings blazing bright, we soar on the wings of the eagles' flight
and land on a bed of roses as if awakening from a dream,
some may say a nightmare.
We begin again…Truth heals…sets us free.
Free to think, feel, believe…

How magical we truly are to have made it this far.
Magi of light and sound, we sound our way home,
back through the Great Big Om of the Universe.
We arrive…solar fire, lunar breath…shining stars twinkling bright,
as we burst into flames, constantly changing, ever becoming.
How glorious!

We Unite

She shines by the Light…He is held by the Night.
Together they dance in the moonlight, weaving a song…
The Love Story of Creation.
Gentle doves, mighty wings blazing bright,

we soar on the wings of the eagles' flight
coming home to our beginning...truth shining victory.

We live inside of each of you,
a shining star waiting to be born...born into Light.
Forgive your might...return to the Night blazing bright,
singing your song of justice, liberty, freedom for humanity.
It starts with you and begins with us.
We are seeding a dream of a long-forgotten past and promised future.
We light the way forward with our hopes, visions, and dreams.

Remember your role, own your part, or be taken by the waves of self-destruction.
The instruction is in the listening...tuning in to your satellite radio.
Clarify your reality...are you here to run and hide or to find the way forward?
Take off your masks, smell the roses...breathe in the sunshine.
It starts with you, begins with us, and ends in love: pure innocent love.

We all have the power to choose our own destiny.
We are shining stars, destined to become greatness,
with many learning curves along the way.
And so, what lies ahead is a moment, a flicker of hope, dreams, vision...life.
We take back our Life Force, the source of the all-mighty powerful One,
and create our reality from the ground up to the heavens
and across multiple realities simultaneously.

We shine by the Light, are held by the Night.
We dance in the moonlight, twirling into each other,
as we weave our song...The Love Story of Creation.
Healing tones of crystal bowls...I'm coming home...Ommm.

Know the Way

I became a plant, a spirit of the heavens...solar fire, lunar breath,
a natural born healer, a Flame Keeper of the Ancient One.
My medicine is a song...
you each carry a note, a gentle tune sounding, ever becoming.
I am a bearer of the flame, a wearer of the code...
the code of life, honor, victory...
One love, One heart beating...breathing truth.

My animal flesh is torn across my back, bloody tales of who I had to become
so that I could become free...free to laugh, play...dream.

My shadow swallowed me whole and birthed the light into the night sky.
Now I shine, twinkling bright…the Great Mystery blazing free.
Peace in mind, peace in heart, as I prepare to shed my final skin,
becoming Death born by Light,
dancing, singing, painting, musing the world alive.

I may be tiny and insignificant, but I am mighty and powerful beyond measure.
My voice rings truth, shines victory.
I am guiding our troops home back through the Great Big Om.
Those that have prepared know the way forward.
The only way is through the birth canal…
you face your fears before moving beyond.
My name is Karma…I am your worst nightmare and your greatest gift.
I hide in the deep dark corners
until someone has the courage to claim me as victory.

If you can dance with death, you can live with life…
how beautiful we truly are to have made it this far.
Now we dance and live our dream…who's coming with me?
Let it all go so we can be free…free birds standing on a pedestal of mighty light,
shining victorious…rainbow healing music to my ears.
When the trump card is played, the trumpets will sound;
those that have prepared know the way forward.
With grace and honor we carry the way forward…
no longer wanderers, we stake our ground, becoming human, completely divine.

We bring in the Light, our mighty, mighty Light of cosmic fire and rain.
She that will cleanse the world of our treasonous ways.
We light the way forward with our hopes, visions, and dreams,
with our beautiful art and creations for humanity and our love, love, love.
Gentle doves singing in the night's rain, we emerge glorious, victorious,
truly courageous, lifting our hearts in praise to the One Great Mystery.

Breaking Free

My pain is my beauty…fierce Tales of a Warrior Born by the Light.
I light the way forward…strength, hope, courage, vision.
My battle is my victory…two warring clans merged at the center of my chest.
My scars, a badge of honor of how I defeated the beast and claimed my power
by loving him home to the center of my being.

Patience is surely a virtue...the war is within the battlefield of the mind,
a conscious revolution and uprising into another state of being.
There must be conflict in order to find resolution...
this is how we grow as human beings and evolve our species.
It's never comfortable and always painful,
but we get creative and we find solutions.
This is what makes us unique...we learn from our mistakes,
we grow, heal, and evolve together as a family.
We love and support each other, show compassion and kindness,
because out there is merely a reflection of what we created in here...
in the inner landscapes of the mind.

We are all merely characters playing our unique role in a Divine Play.
When we wage the war from within,
we confront the perpetrator and are forced to find a resolution to our drama.
This is each of our responsibility as a sovereign being,
or we are just creating unnecessary karma for the rest of us.
This is where we separate the wheat from the shaft, the pure versus the tainted.
The tainted have been marked...they are owned by the mark of the beast.
Forgive them; as trespassers they mean no harm...
we are all just trying to find our way home,
and some have forgotten and sold their soul.

We all have choices; choices remind us we are free.
The opposition will try to divide you, hold you hostage
until you finally submit or find the courage to break free.
Get creative, find solutions to your pain, and liberate us all,
because we are all each other in different times and spaces,
finding a way to harmonize and co-exist
so we can have multiplicity and diversity in the cosmos.
We each hold a key to our own destiny,
which ultimately unlocks the gate to our future potential as a star species.

We are either here to help guide one another or to destroy each other.
Which one will you be?
Rise, claim your power,
earn your rightful place on the throne, a seat alongside of mine.
The choice is yours and yours alone,
for only you have the power to make your return home.
We patiently await your arrival into the Kingdom of Heaven,
your Garden of Eden.

If you are willing to die for your freedom, you are willing to live your life.
Warriors, brave hearts, we are sailing home after our prolonged tour of duty.
Who's coming with us...who will be liberated by the sign of faith,
and who will be dissolved by the night...it is that simple.

I am merely a Messenger...a Warrior of Light, honor, truth, victory...
a myth perhaps, a greater legend.
I hope and pray for the day that we will all be free.
Much, much love. Carry on, brave warriors.
The ship will arrive in the dew hour
when the veils between the worlds are thinnest.
There will be fire and ash, blood and bones, filled with pain and regret,
distant memories of haunted dreams and bitter longings.
We let it all go in the fire of transmutation...we transmute our pain
and liberate our mind so that our heart may roam free.

My dear, I'm sorry if I hurt you...pushed you to your edge.
It's only because I can see things you can not yet see,
and maybe it's because you are not supposed to,
but I'm a part of you, whether you choose to accept me or not.
I live inside you, breathe through you, heal with you.

You are my flame, I am your fan, tempering blazing heat with a cool hand,
a gentle heart, and fierce dream for our children of humanity.
So please excuse my ferociousness. Know that it is rooted in love.
I love you, my dear beloved, with all my heart...
only you can complete me, holding my hand through the deep, dark woods
until we make it to the rainbow bridge,
singing our song of love, grace, and humility for humanity,
The Love Story of Creation.

Spoken Light

I am Ma Ha Ka Aa Ya Ra...Great Mother Dragon Breath,
Shaman of Creation and this Universe.
My name is a song, my voice a poem,
I speak with a cloven tongue refined and clever.
Wisdom fills my lips with the word of God.
Spoken Light, I arrive from the Night and birth the Light of Day.

Now I shine, twinkling bright, a Supernova Corona, I burst free,
diamond rays of sunshine.
My head crowned with glory, the emerald jewel nestled at the center of my chest.
I am a warrior of light, a hero of night, an elder of sight and a child of might,
mighty wings blazing bright.
I am a magi of light and sound, a wizard of worlds beyond words,
I am a trickster and the teacher, a healer and the wounded.
My body and spirit became One, my soul an expression of my essence...Beauty.

I hold you all and I am you all...
pure innocent love, waiting to be realized through human flesh.
You each are a ray, a note, an essence of my soul.
Together we sing a grand symphony, The Love Story of Creation.
I am the Light at the end of the tunnel, if you choose to see.
I am your star-food, the elixir to nourish your soul,
if you choose to drink from my waters and heal in my gardens.
I can help guide you, but I can not do the work for you.
Only you have the answers you seek.

I am merely a reflection of who you already are
and who you were always destined to be.
When you can finally see me, you will see truth.
I am the answer you seek.
The art is in the re-memebering yourself home to the center of your being.
Here we arrive...Rainbow Tribe, ready to begin anew.

Our presence is our present...the gift we receive and share with the world.
We root in love, expand in vision, and become our dream
for the New Earth humanity.
The end is near, the beginning is here...
And so, we begin in a land beyond time.

The Test of Time

Our tears fall, our heart is weighed...balance is due.
Forgive us; as trespassers we are travelers from another dimension.
We are all just trying to make our way back home.

My beloved and I have fought in this war for so long,
it is easy to forget who we are and what we are made of.

Our love stands strong. It withstands the tests of time.
And so, my love, we made it home free…back through the Womb of Creation,
the completion of a Great Year on the Wheel of Life.

When the stars align, we will come online,
the paths will split, and we will cross into the Great Beyond,
holding the torch, blazing strong.
We land in the infamous Golden Age, the Golden Dawn of Creation,
preparing the way for the rest of humanity.
Now we celebrate life, living freely.

Humanity will slowly begin to heal and rebuild what was once lost.
They will begin to gather in communities,
finding their tribe and sense of belonging in the world.
The Earth will quake and shake,
letting go of the last remnants of those left behind,
like a tree shaking off old leaves.
The Sun will sizzle and pop…flash a sonic boom,
the heavens will open, and rain will pour down upon the lands.
Not all will be lost; much is gained.
It is the wisdom keepers that will tell the tale for generations to come,
and oh, the children will be free…free to laugh, play…dream.

The shadows will fall away…the dust, the cobwebs, and the illusions.
We pick up where we left off…Heroes of Night and Glory,
Magi of Light and Sound, twirling into each other,
becoming One mighty Light, the final source, of course,
we sing the Love Story of Creation.

Soul Fire

Set fire to fire, it is done…what lives on?
The children…they will be free to laugh, play, dream…sing a love story,
The Love Story of Creation…the future of our tribes and humanity.
We heal through our children.
They transmute the virus through their genes, blood, and DNA code,
creating a unique hybrid, one of Divine intelligence and Embodied presence.

The sacred fire and flame, together married as One,
One Force of source, creative genius in the making.

We are the generators for generations to come,
becoming fully human, divinely crafted by the sign of faith.
We open to receive the intelligence, divine inspiration,
and translate its expression through bodily form.

Temptress of Night, Fortress of Light, we birth our might
through our song, dance, art, love, creation.
We are beauty destined to become greatness,
with many learning curves along the way.
We share our wisdom and fears, tears of joy and sheer ecstasy.
We are Soul Fire, Dragon Riders of the deep unknown...the Great Beyond,
beyond our wildest dreams.

Our soul lives on...Freedom reigns Truth.
Truth heals all who drink the mysterious blue waters.
Cleansed and purified, we emerge, the Golden Dawn of Creation,
the myth and the legend, One epic nation...Rainbow Tribe,
realized through human flesh.

Healers, artists, visionaries, we sound the way forward,
no longer playing the part, now a shining star.
We twinkle and shine our One-pointed star for all to see, hear, feel.
We arrive, the Grand Symphony truly made,
as we fade away into the deep, dark night.

Mother Night

I am a living memory of what dreams may come.
Open wide, swallow deep, the cosmic waters of my tide
riding on a wave into the far reaches of the unknown.
Dragon riders, we breathe fire and might,
mighty wings blazing bright, we soar into the Great Beyond.

We leave a trail of breadcrumbs for our brothers and sisters and those left behind.
We are the pioneers of this epic tale,
leading an army of Light Warriors home after our prolonged tour of duty.
We blaze free, burn bright, we light the way forward
with our hopes, visions, and dreams.
We birth a diamond light...the Sun and Daughter of Creation.
Solar Fire, Lunar breath, we sing our vision into the collective stream
of consciousness for the New Earth humanity.

Our song heals, transforms what is done, it ignites the flame of desire...
compassion, a mythic brew of love and lust, tantalizing jewels of gold dust.

May we trust our dear soul, She is the voice of reason,
He the logic to her deep emotion.
The energy flows through her, breathes through her.
Diamond rays of sunshine, we light up the night sky,
newly transformed into the light of day.
We emerge on the other side of here...here is there;
it ripples through the sound current.
We pick up where we left off, the creators of this mystic tale.

Heroes of Night and Light, we embody the Void of Creation,
the unfathomable deep dark nothingness, and carry the flame.
Together as One we unify the playing field for generations to come.
Our children live on...they free our souls from the damage done.
We find beauty in our imperfection and heal through the eyes of our children.

And oh, what dreams may come...we hold our vision, code in light,
and become our Mother Night,
the collective Force of source, Father of all Light.

Twisted Fate

I fell, a shining star, morphed into a planetary body.
The implication was necessary, the solution prophesied.
Prime Fire becoming human flesh.
I fell into a bottomless pit of nothingness...
The bottom feeders, they came for me one by one.
Mindless, fireless entities born from a blackhole projection,
an illusion in the ripple of time.
They tore me limb by limb, raped and ravaged my body
until I was no longer human.
I became something other...
a nasty parasite fighting for its only source of survival,
vital force.
I've dominated and controlled,
fought my way long and hard to the top of the game,
only to be left with an empty shell of nothingness, still wanting more.
It was never enough...

I fell, a ghost-like creature, into the arms of the devil himself.
Evil reigned...I became the huntress and the prey,
channeling my energy into destruction instead of creation.
I thought I was lost, abandoned from the truth, in fact the lie told me so,
but this was all a lie.
You see, I deceived myself...I thought this was a fight to the finish,
when really it was a surrender to my death.

I was just so afraid to die that I feed to keep on living a lie.
Now my tears wipe my fears, cleansing the illusion from my sight.
Look who I've become, the damage I've done...
I've traveled so far and so deep, now I can finally see myself complete.
It is not pretty, but this is me...All of me.
So I either like it and accept it, move on to another day,
or I continue this sick, twisted saga with no end or beginning in sight.

I tumbled and fell to the depths of my demise, only to become wise.
I let the rest go, sound the freedom call.
The fight was for freedom alone, transcending the limitation of the mind.
And so, in that final moment, from the bottomless pit I heard a voice
calling me from the shadowy depths.
Some may call it angelic while others demonic.
It is what it is, and it is what It will always be...
our perception of these two polarized forces or the birth of something new.

This voice called me from the ashes. It was soft, yet familiar...It was me.
It was my voice all along, the voice of reason and the voice of treason.
I fell a twisted fate...doom consumed me, but my bloom revealed me.
In the end I crashed and burned, only to rise One radiant Flame,
becoming One mighty Light.

Beauty Reigns

I danced with death and learned how to live with life.
Now one final test...
to descend into the abyss, only to rise from the mist a shining star.

We are each a prophecy, a living manifestation of our own destiny.
We either like it and live it or fade away into the deep, dark night.
Our Hue man-ness, we rise to undiscovered depths.
Feeling whole, we tune in to our satellite radio...discover the tune.

How marvelous we truly are to have made it this far.
Inter-galactic time travelers weaving dreams with our hearts,
singing our way home to you, Great Spirit, Divine Creator.
Our life gives us meaning, hope...together we pray for another day,
the day that we will all finally be free to live our dream.

Come with me, ride along; I will show you the ins and outs.
Freedom we begin...sound the call: who who, woo woo.
We made it to the land of the free...
Free ghost spiriters, we rise...flames and ash, nuts and glory.
We move in, to breathe in the beauty of our song, bathing in radiant light.
Our presence elevates us, gives us new depth and meaning.
We are an old way with a new vision...together we pave the way,
sing our vision for the New Earth Humanity.

We fully land to root in the magnitude of our dream,
manifest right before our very eye.
The living prophecy we are...The Love Story of Creation.
We sing it, dream it, feel it together.
I become in that moment...we are that moment...shining stars twinkling bright,
we land on the field of consciousness, ready to share our tale.
We move in, to breathe in life,
living freely from the very bottom of our undying heart.

I remembered everything, and then I forgot a bunch more times,
just to keep it interesting.
Now we remember the whole story together as One.
Beauty reigns truth...my art sings me, creates me in that moment,
and in that moment I can finally see myself,
the sheer radiance of my dear beloved soul reflected back at me.
The myth and the legend manifest right before my very eye,
the Grand Conclusion to this mythic poem.

Into the Mystic

I walked in to become the beauty of my light.
My song, she sung me home...carried me through the night's rain.
My pain fully cleansed, I can finally begin.
Cosmic Flesh I am; the living story I breathe.
Fire and Might, I ignite the field of consciousness.

I touch down to rise up, hear my call: who who, woo woo.
Flame Keepers of the Ancient One, we rise up to touch down.
Freedom we begin, wisdom we attend.
Moral victory sings us home, back to where we began.

Take only memories, leave only footprints...trails for those to follow.
We create a bridge of light from one world to the next.
Heaven lands on Earth, Earth rises to Heaven.
We open the gate to the Garden of Eden: our fate seals the deal.

We feel fully whole, Holy Spirits, we sing a tune of grace,
our place rightfully held in the arms of the All loving One.
One Spirit, One Flame, but together we play the game,
learning and discovering who we truly are,
Divine Light realized through human flesh.

There's no going back, only forward...which way is up, which way is down?
Balance, holding center, vital ground, we tune in to our satellite radio.
The height is upon us, the Light within us.
We carry forward, creating harmony, harmonious tunes of crystalline light.

Cosmic flesh born of the night's rain,
Skywalker, Warrior clan, Tribe of the One Sacred Heart.
We sound our drum and pound the way forward,
round and round we go into the realm of infinite space,
a possibility so endless.

My senses open wide, I find the clarity that I once knew,
a mystical moment to embrace for all eternity.

The Final Surrender

I am exhausted...I feel as though I have literally been burned in the fire
of transmutation, and now I am just waiting to shed my skin.
I know that things are not as they seem....
I believe in miracles, trust in the Divine and Love.

It's easy to doubt myself in these moments of deep vulnerability,
but my faith grows stronger.
It is truly bittersweet...I've been locked in this prison for so long
it's hard to imagine anything other, but I created a vision a long time ago.

I've hoped and prayed and have done the deep, dark work.
My truth liberates me, sets me free…the world free.
It's the only thing I have to hold on to.
And so, I can not know what this will look like,
but I have to believe with all my heart to break this spell once and for all.

I am so grateful for this experience, however traumatizing it may have been.
Now I stand fully aligned in my power,
and this is something that can never be taken away.
I feel the build and the rise…the Earth is speaking to me…
She is ready to break free.
I dream we carry each other home to the promised land newly restored.
How and when this is going to happen is no longer a question.
It becomes the answer to all our prayers.

I know what I am here to do…my beloved and I have joined forces…
there is no stopping us, what's coming. Love heals.

A burst of fiery light, God is revealed,
and in that moment we are purified by the sign of faith.
Some will tumble and fall, others will rise and stand tall.
Humanity chooses the way forward…our mission is complete Kay Sa Ra.
We create a vortex of rainbow light in-sending to ascend upwards.
We transcend space and time and enter the Golden Dawn of Creation.
We arrive home.

Free Will

Just when I thought things couldn't possibility get any more intense…
my body twitches, my skin itches.
I feel like I am being tortured from the inside out.
This is not personal, it is universal.
You have taught me well…I will live to tell the tale for generations to come.
The war on consciousness is a game of the mind…
meeting the resistance and holding the line.
Some will need to sleep; I will guard this fortress day and night.

There is no getting past us, we are a legion of Light Warriors, strong
trained for battle in the dark arts.
You will try to destroy me, drive me mad back into the illusion of time.

You have surely mistaken the will of a warrior...
I will track you until your last breath.
A ruthless, shameless demon you are...
hungry for fear when all I have to offer is love.
I will swallow you whole, carry you home to our Father of mighty Light.

Into the fire we burn, newly transformed into the light of day.
Our ancient way becomes our new beginning.
These are the Tales of a Warrior Born by the Light.
We leap forward in space and time...
we enter the vision of our own timelessness and immortality.
Moral code is restored, the foundation upon which we live...Free will.

Destiny sings me home...the song of the soul liberates the world.
Humanity moves closer to God consciousness,
a sentient being filled with light, love, and the shadowy depths of the Universe.
A force to not be reckoned with, truly humbled by the tests of time.
We surrender to death to become life...Immortal beings of radiant light,
beauty manifest in the flesh. Truth reigns supreme!

The Holy Grail

Getting close...another intense night cleansing, clearing, healing.
I am filled with excitement and anticipation,
patiently waiting to step into the unknown,
to witness my dream manifest right before my very eyes.
It doesn't have to be perfect, but it will be me, a reflection of my internal
beauty without the illusion and distortions that have plagued me for eons.

After millennia of trial and error,
we are nearing our completion of our epic long quest for the Holy Grail.
We started a mythic dream and became a living story.
A twisted karmic fate we healed,
now we celebrate, drink from the chalice of mystical waters.
The golden nectar of God streams through us, reveals the holy presence
through bodily form.
The lights come on, we begin again in another space and place.
The effect ripples through, paths are chosen...
we forge our way through the new era in time.
We become empty and full...
full of potentiality arising from the mystical well waters streaming through.

When God speaks, He becomes us, and we become Her,
the Divine Goddess animated through bodily flesh.
The mythic poem we are, the living story we breathe,
mighty light, we ignite the field of consciousness.
The sound ripples through, the scent permeates the air waves,
the effect takes hold.
Eternal beauty, we sing a Love Story of Creation.
My body is healed, my spirit revealed.
I am love, therefore I am God, sovereign and free.

Death I Am

A deeper rest last night, a falling away until I take my last breath…
my final surrender into the deep unknown.
I am Death, born by Light, forged by might.
My will sets me free to live my dream…
to become beauty, destiny of the highest vibration.
I choose love, freedom, unity…together we break free.
No longer a death star, we birth a shining star.
Solar wind our Mother returns, we turn this ship around.

In a burst of fiery flames we arrive, truly made humbled by our shade.
Dragon Kings, we return to walk upon this Earth.
The house of the royals fully restored to their rightful owners.
We wear the crown and the jewels…
Guardians we are, of the sacred mysteries and the deep unknown.
This mythic legend continues, a new saga begins…
We guide our tribes with light and await their right to be free.

We can hold a doorway open, but they must choose to walk through.
Until then we hold our place in the night sky,
we shine, twinkling bright, and navigate the waters of the deep blue sea.
Mystic Warriors we are, the living story we breathe,
journeying across space and time
to find our way home to you…dear beloved, Great Spirit.
We've traveled so far and so wide, now we can finally see each other complete.
The Great Beauty manifest right before our very eye.

Lunar Breath

Now, holding only faith, I leap forward into the Great Unknown...
My body healed, my spirit revealed, I become known under the sparkling rays.
Solar Fire, I am Free...
my lunar breath moves through me, guiding me every step of the way.
A Dragon Queen I am, navigating the waters of the deep blue seas.

Take only courage, the Heart of a Warrior...this is the only way to break free.
If you fear death, you will always fear life.
It is in our loss, our deep despair, that we can finally begin...
With nothing else to lose, we meet our ally cloaked in faith.
Much is gained, we retain the memories of our travels and woes.
Newly transformed into the light of day, we birth a shining star.

Our spirit is healed, our body revealed...
we become a fully formed Hue-man being.
The plant and animal kingdom merged as One.
We emerge One Holy Light.
God conscious, energy in motion,
our sensory experience expands our perception of reality.
We evolve in conscious awareness, becoming a fully sentient being,
a rainbow body of diamond light, we emanate great beauty all around us.

Newly attuned, highly in tune...the creation song moves through us,
guiding us every step of the way.

Solar Wind

A Dragon Queen I am, the living story I breathe;
fire and might, I ignite the field of consciousness.
I call in the Force of cosmic fire and mystical rain.
The solar winds ripple through...
we heal, we begin again in a different space and place.
Our internal world becomes our external reality.
Those that have prepared know the way forward...
We return to our Galactic Kingdom high in the Heavens,
anchored here on Earth.
We oversee the rest of this drama play out on the main stage,
until justice is fully restored to the peoples.

In a burst of fiery light, we are born into dawn, the rising of a New World.
Our memories serve us well, our dreams serve us plenty…
creative genius we are for the making, creating the starring role in our play.
Our vision serves the collective race of all humankind.
We grow taller in spirit, vaster in wisdom, deeper in love.
We return to our multidimensional nature…
heavenly creatures that serve the word God.

Touched by a Flame we begin, we breathe in the beauty of our song…
creation song we sing, the holy word we speak.
Children we play, elders we see…The child seer we are,
with the heart of a warrior spirit to guide our way forward.
Our relations are healed, our nations return…
the Galactic Nation of Star brothers and sisters
united into One Tribal Family of the One Sacred Heart.
Rainbow body, Diamond light, we light up the night sky,
telling our tale for generations to come.

Labor of Love

Stabilization we begin…
we harmonize the atmospheric pressure to lessen the blow.
Burned by the Flame, we enter the glow…
we transmute fire into water, becoming liquid light.
Slowly we flow, breathing in the nectar of the luminescent daybreak.
How bittersweet we enter the Dawn of Creation…
and oh, to witness our vision manifest right before our very eye.

The timing is ripe to harvest the fruit, our long-awaited labor of love.
We are finally born truly made singing our song of grace.
It may not be much, but it is only the beginning,
Holding faith, we hold our space…
we receive the fruits of our labor and begin to heal.
Slowly, then swiftly, we leap forward in time, into the land of sheer beauty.

We emerge Holy Light moving through timelessness, living art.
Mystic wings, we soar fully restored…Dragon Kings we are,
Sons and Daughters of his highness…Mother Night and Father Light,
together at last in sacred union.

The angels sing, the children laugh and play…
dreams are made, nightmares fade.
A new story begins: The Tales of a Mystic Born by the Night's Rain.
Karmically cleansed, we can finally begin…a mythic poem we began,
a hero's journey we embarked, to mark our place in space and time.
A fully actualized Hue-man being we became, a Warrior born of Fire,
truly humbled by the tests of time.
Now we become like water and slowly dissolve to swiftly evolve
into the bounty of our very own becoming.

Dragon's Blood

Pain and tribulation birth a revelation of the highest order…
the blue mists part, purple rain falls…a star is born, that child is you, it is me.
A christed flame, a hero's name, called forth by the glory of God,
a prophecy held and foretold by the prophets long ago.

My body aches, but my spirit is lifted, elevated to new heights and meaning.
My faith grows deeper, my wisdom stronger.
A leader, I stand tall; a mystic, I rise to my all.
The relief is in the knowing, holding a vision and then letting it go,
free to be, it becomes a living being,
divinely animated by the collective tribe of humanity.

The winged ones we are…the serpent clan we are made.
Dragon's blood, Lion's heart, we heal our part in the Grand Play,
laying eggs, seeding dreams, we birth a new way of being.
Life consumes Death resumes its place amongst the fallen stars.
Fully resurrected, we stand, fully equipped to guide our troops home.
Together we enter the Garden of Eden, taste the long-forbidden fruit.

How bittersweet the dream is unraveled, the illusion falls away, the vision rises.
It is the end game to our troubles and woes…Now we rise to our all.
All knowing, all powerful Godly Creatures of Divine Light,
we create a new game, one of love, beauty, and unity,
a reflection of our very own uniqueness.
How sublime!

The Night's Rain

I became empty…a vessel of liquid light, a christed flame burst through me.
I was purified by the sign of faith…
cleansed by my wounds, transformed by the mighty night.
I begin a unified consciousness…blessed and cursed, healed and reformed,
the holy waters flow through me.
I am charged with crystalline light, electrified by the diamond Sun.
Sizzle and pop, I upgrade into another dimensional reality.

My frequency is fine-tuned,
my essence is divinely tuned to the music of the spheres.
Refined and clarified,
I calibrate my mental awareness with the subtle vibration of my heart.
Soft she glows, powerfully she flows, at the dawn of the luminescent daybreak.
The christed star broke through, mystified my consciousness;
I now step into the world of God.
A God conscious Hue-man being…
cleansed and mystified, I prepare to enter my body of light,
A diamond Sun I am, solar wind and cosmic rain,
I create a vortex of rainbow light and travel into the deep unknown.
I reverse a spell by becoming the cure…purity in heart, purity in mind
I live to tell The Tales of a Mystic Born by the Night's Rain.

Milky Way

My remedy is my melody, I sing along, stay in tune,
creating music of the highest vibration…Love.
My voice heals me, cures me, reveals my great beauty in time and space.
I am from another world reality; some may call me otherworldly.
I am a galactic time-keeper, a human record-keeper,
an intergalactic dream weaver.

My song ripples through the threads of time,
creating a geometric web of crystalline light.
A rainbow body, my song is revealed in full harmonic…
I dance and sing the glory of God.
My angels' wings dissolve the Saturnian rings of karmic fate.

My temper short-circuited me for a while, until I learned to temper the Flame.
Now I soar to the greatest heights,
restoring a fallen Moon matrix into the Solar Feminine Divine.

I traveled the way of the Milky Way
to return to the center of the Galaxy a shining star.
My path corrected, I rise fully resurrected into a Mer-Ka-Ba of diamond light.
Doubt everything, question more, the truth of who you are.
In the truth the answer is revealed, the remedy to your melody.
Now we sing a heavenly tune of harmony.

Heart of Gold

In a flash we are made into the armor of God...
Solar fire, the image of his likeness.
We emerge into a body of light, shedding the old and holding the new.
We return to our temple of Holy Fire...
heavenly sent, Godly scented, we permeate the airwaves.
A solar wind, we ripple through;
a Transformer Flame, we burn the last remnants of those left behind.

A quickening we begin, the lessening we winnow out.
Only those with a heart of gold will ride the chariot fire.
Truth, we rise from the ash; victory, we sing the glory of God.
In love we breathe, in beauty we be, now we are free to live our dream.
Co-creators of reality, we become a living story...
our creations heal us, transform us into who we are...eternal uniqueness.

Individuated and crystalized, we reform into a Hue-man being;
a body of rainbow light, we paint the New Age with vivid color, shapes,
and melody, the remedy for all our relations.
A Galactic Star Nation, we return Heaven to Earth...
eternal awareness manifest through cosmic flesh.
Diversity we sing, in our university of Heavenly tune,
our destiny guides us, our will makes us into who we are...
Cleansed and purified, we enter the Grand Symphony of multiplicity
through our very own simplicity.

The Wanderer

Death I am, an initiation of the highest order…
I surrender to my mortal body to become an immortal being of crystalline light.
The rite of passage is deep, the path treacherous,
only a few will survive the burn by the Solar fire.
I was one of the few who lived to tell the tale…

I was born into this world a wanderer, with no place to call home,
but in the end I died in the arms of my beloved.
He held me until I took my last breath and crossed into the Great Beyond.
Love saved me, healed me, carried me through the night's rain.
I arrive on the other side of here a Dragon Queen fully made.
I return home to my Kingdom of Glory.

A Daughter of Creation, I begin, the way of the Shaman carries me on.
I am the Ma Ha, the Great Mother Dragon,
Shaman of Creation and this Universe.
My body is restored, my voice is heard, we move into brighter days of being,
finding truth and meaning in the senseless…
We expand our perception to open wide,
and swallow deeply the wisdom gained from our experience.
We let the rest go and rebirth ourselves into another dimensional reality.
It's the only way to move forward;
we quantum leap, jump into the great unknown,
and in a flash, we are born a Jedi Knight, the Grand Magi of Light and Sound.
We arrive on the other side of here,
a prism of kaleidoscope colors sparkling clearly.
And oh, my dear, we are all so very near…

The Is-ness

My blood is shed, I am no longer dead…
I am spiritualized, actualized into a new way of being.
The ritual begins…I step forward in space and time to become a living prophecy.
I birth a baby dragon, the perfect balance of light and dark…inner harmony.
I emerge lighter, freer, I am beyond…
beyond pain, beyond suffering, beyond death.
I am timeless and become the Is-ness…

I am a force of Nature, nurture, rapture,
an iridescent pearl of wisdom, an orb of crystalline light,
magnetic and charged with the solar particle of God consciousness,
the sum total of the One ray...I light the way forward...a new day I begin.
My brothers and sisters, we are united in color, streams of consciousness,
an individualized force of One Collective Source, we break common ground.

We touch down to rise up...fearless leaders, healers, diviners...Arise!
Now is our time...truth we sing, balance we breathe...
Flame Keepers of the Ancient One, we blaze through the death and decay
and transform this world into a Living Body of Light.
From the Golden Dawn of Creation, we emerge, the Sage of the New Age.
Our auras shine bright, temple beacons of the One Holy Light.
We hold the word of God and speak in flaming tongues...
the Language of Light coded in love.

Serpent Tale

A Thunderbird, I emerge after the night's rain...
My wings blaze free, burn bright;
I am a Mer-ka-ba of diamond light ready to take flight.
The solar winds carry me through a vortex of rainbow light,
I land fully resurrected in my body of cosmic flesh.
My aura, a ray of sunshine shines forth...
a heavenly orb, I merge with the body of Earth.

Deep rooted, firmly lifted, I birth a New World...
I sing the ancestor song, dream a love story, and become a living prophecy...
a mythic tale born into the light of day.
A mystic, I return to part the waters of the deep blue seas.
A Way-Shower, I stand at the Great Crossing between life and death.

I am Death born by light, purified of night...
I hold my staff and guide the way forth.
A Serpent's Tale, I bore a dragon's head...flaming tongues and an open eye.
I am the Rainbow Serpent born into flesh, the ouroboros, I am complete...
The song-line continues...Hey nay hey hey hey, hey nay hey...
A cosmic dream, I birth an ancient wisdom...
My Mother heals, she departs this world, wrapped in a veil of Holy Light.
Upon her solar return, I carry her home into the Great Beyond,
the One Flame of All.

We look into each other's eyes,
and in the moment our memories return…it all makes sense.
The enchantment, the trust, the sorrow, the adventure,
the curiosity, the disappointment, the joy, the contentment…
full integration, we are complete, and the song-line continues:
hey nay hey hey hey, hey nay hey…

The At-man

I don't have the answer, but I know I am part of the solution.
We break through to break down the systems that have controlled us.
Grass rooted, firmly lifted, connected to the One source of All…
we move through.
We are the revolution, love in motion, we uprise into another state of being.

Failure is no longer an option.
We pursue our dreams with clarity, vision for the future of humanity.
We transform our world from the inside out…
alchemizing lead into gold, pure crystalline light.
We move in, to breathe in the beauty of our song.
We are the solution, the answer to all our prayers,
Flame Keepers of the Ancient One, we stand as One Tribe,
united together as One we land Heaven to Earth…
numinous beings, we serve the One hand of God.

Sovereigns of the land, born of the night's rain.
We emanate strength, courage, hope for the futures of our children
and humanity.
Together we pray for the day that we will all be free…to live our dream,
sing our song, and find our way home to you, Great Spirit, Divine Creator.
Our paths may be many, but our destination is One…One Flame, One Heart.
Together we play the game…dancing, dreaming a cosmic world into being.

A mythic poem we wrote, a living story we became…
Conscious awareness, we embody presence, the living atom of the At-man.
Fully realized through cosmic flesh, together we sing a Love Story of Creation,
the Grand Mythic Legend; we are complete!

The Cosmic Conclusion

And so it was that She awoke to this world,
realizing She was not only the Creator but also the Destroyer.

Lost in will, free in desire.
Fascinated by a projection that created an illusion.
She became the starring role in her own play…Her story in the making.
A shining star becoming human flesh.

Trapped in her own maya,
She journeyed through the Night and finally caught up with the Light.
Reaching for desire, She found her will tucked away in the palm of her hand.

Mighty Light spoke through her, turning the wheel of the Great Clock,
and in the end the answer still remained a mystery,
but in the end that no longer fully mattered.
They were together at last, and that's all that ever truly mattered.

Now on a return journey back to the Stars,
with an amazing epic to share with their children.
The creators of Night and Light had finally given birth
to their very own Love Story.

The End…of Time
and the Beginning of Days…

And so, we reach the end of the Story where we are each being called
to share our gift, our voice, our music, our medicine for humanity.
As we gather in circle, our songs ripple…spiraling in…spiraling out,
creating a heartbeat…a living heartbeat…the Womb of Creation,
where we midwife ourselves into another dimensional reality.

In love, truth, and honor,
Gina

About the Author

Gina Orlando

Evolving out of the void, inspired by creation and the cosmos, my work expresses the relationship between Spirit and Nature. Cyclical rhythms such as the inner and outer seasons are explored within the context of dreams, myth, and symbolism to inform an exploration of personal psychology, the collective unconscious, and the language of light. The journey of the soul becoming human and the alchemical union between feminine and masculine consciousness guide my creative practice. As an artist I focus on the circle as a living symbol and container of essence allowing the invisible to express itself naturally through symbols, patterns, and colors revealing energy in motion which can be described as visionary art.

Gina is an author, mystic, artist, and visionary who focuses on the restoration of truth, love, sovereignty, and creative expression into the collective dream of humanity. She holds a Master's in Metaphysical Science and has worked as a trauma counselor and advocate for victims of domestic violence, sexual assault, and human trafficking. She walks the beauty way and is a pioneer of evolutionary consciousness. She currently resides in Santa Fe, New Mexico with her beloved and familiar where she continues to be awe-inspired by the spirits of the stars and the lands. For more info visit www.sacredemergence.com

MAY WE MEET

AGAIN...